Home Office Research Study 283

Are special measures working? Evidence from surveys of vulnerable and intimidated witnesses

Becky Hamlyn, Andrew Phelps, Jenny Turtle and Ghazala Sattar

The views expressed in this report are those of the authors, not necessarily those of the Home Office (nor do they reflect Government policy).

Home Office Research, Development and Statistics Directorate
June 2004

Home Office Research Studies

The Home Office Research Studies are reports on research undertaken by or on behalf of the Home Office. They cover the range of subjects for which the Home Secretary has responsibility. Other publications produced by the Research, Development and Statistics Directorate include Findings, Statistical Bulletins and Statistical Papers.

The Research, Development and Statistics Directorate

RDS is part of the Home Office. The Home Office's purpose is to build a safe, just and tolerant society in which the rights and responsibilities of individuals, families and communities are properly balanced and the protection and security of the public are maintained.

RDS is also part of National Statistics (NS). One of the aims of NS is to inform Parliament and the citizen about the state of the nation and provide a window on the work and performance of government, allowing the impact of government policies and actions to be assessed.

Therefore –

Research Development and Statistics Directorate exists to improve policy making, decision taking and practice in support of the Home Office purpose and aims, to provide the public and Parliament with information necessary for informed debate and to publish information for future use.

First published 2004
Application for reproduction should be made to the Communications and Development Unit, Room 264, Home Office, 50 Queen Anne's Gate, London SW1H 9AT.
© Crown copyright 2004   ISBN 1 84473 285.1
                          ISSN 0072 6435

Foreword

This report presents the findings of surveys of vulnerable and intimidated witnesses which looked at experiences and satisfaction before and after the implementation of special measures under the Youth Justice and Criminal Evidence Act 1999. Vulnerable and intimidated witnesses attending all Crown Courts and magistrates' courts where a Witness Service was operating were approached to take part in the research.

The post implementation survey showed that most witnesses using special measures rated them very highly, and around a third of witnesses using them said they would not otherwise have been able or willing to give evidence. Vulnerable and intimidated witnesses were found to be less satisfied with their overall experience of the criminal justice system than witnesses more generally, although there was a statistically significant increase in satisfaction ratings between the pre- and post-implementation surveys. Satisfaction was higher with individual criminal justice agencies than with the criminal justice system overall; it was particularly high for Witness Service, court staff and judges/magistrates.

Giving evidence can probably never be made pleasant, but the survey findings suggest that special measures are helping to improve witness experience and satisfaction with the criminal justice system.

Tony Munton
Assistant Director
Research, Development and Statistics Directorate

Acknowledgements

We would like to thank the many people who assisted in the production of this report. Particular thanks are due to members of the Home Office steering group.

The survey was undertaken by BMRB Social Research, and we would like to thank all staff who have provided help and support in the organisation of questionnaire distribution, fieldwork and data analysis.

We would especially like to thank Victim Support gave invaluable assistance in recruiting respondents.

Finally, many thanks to all those who gave up their time to be interviewed for the survey.

Becky Hamlyn
Andrew Phelps
Jenny Turtle
Ghazala Sattar

Contents

List of tables

List of figures

Summary

Background

In 1998 the report of the Inter-Departmental Group on the Treatment of Vulnerable and Intimidated Witnesses in the Criminal Justice System, entitled *Speaking Up For Justice* (Home Office 1998), made 78 recommendations to improve the treatment of vulnerable and intimidated witnesses (VIWs) within the Criminal Justice System (CJS) and enable them to give best evidence. Measures requiring legislation were included in the Youth Justice and Criminal Evidence Act 1999. Other measures required administrative action and training.

The 1999 Act makes available a range of 'special measures', which are set out in Part II, Chapter 1 (sections 23-30), which are aimed at helping VIWs give best evidence. Vulnerable witnesses are defined in the legislation as:

- all witnesses aged under 17;

- witnesses with a physical disability[1];

- witnesses with a mental disorder or otherwise with a significant impairment of intelligence or social functioning (learning disability - see footnote 1); and

- witnesses likely to suffer fear or distress about testifying, including victims of sexual offences and witnesses who fear or suffer intimidation (see footnote 1).

The special measures are: screening the witness from the accused; giving evidence by live television link; removal of wigs and gowns in court; video-recorded evidence-in-chief; video recorded cross- or re-examination; examination through an intermediary; clearing the public gallery; and provision of aids to communication. Other measures were also introduced which did not require legislation. These included: pre-court familiarisation visits; the presence of a supporter in court; escorts to and from court; liaison officers; separate waiting areas; and the use of pagers.

The majority of special measures were introduced in the Crown Court in July 2002, although video-recorded cross- and re-examination, and examination through an

---

1   Where the court considers the quality of evidence given by the witness is likely to be diminished by this reason.

intermediary, are yet to be implemented. Implementation in magistrates' courts was restricted to use of live TV links and video-recorded evidence-in-chief for child witnesses. A wider range of measures is expected to be rolled out in 2004/5.

Because of the major significance of these changes, it was considered essential to assess their impact. An important aspect of the research that was commissioned in consequence was to seek the views of VIWs themselves about their experiences of the CJS and, in particular, of giving evidence. Surveys were undertaken with samples of VIWs prior to the implementation of the new provisions (the phase 1 survey – this took place between November 2000 and February 2001) and after the provisions had been introduced and had had time to 'bed in' (the phase 2 survey – this took place between April and June 2003). The surveys covered all four groups of VIWs listed above.

Objectives

Specifically, the objectives of the phase 1 and 2 surveys were:

1. to determine whether the introduction of the new measures has been accompanied by an increase in VIWs' satisfaction with the CJS;

2. to investigate to what extent the provision of support for VIWs has changed in practice with the implementation of special measures; and

3. to explore VIWs' attitudes to the measures.

The first of these objectives has a strong bearing on assessing progress towards achieving the CJS Public Service Agreement (PSA) target of improving public confidence in the CJS, including increasing the satisfaction of victims and witnesses (Home Office, 2003).

Methods

In phase 1, VIWs were recruited at all Crown Courts and magistrates' courts where a Witness Service operated between October and December 2000. Because data are not routinely recorded on all witness vulnerabilities, the Witness Service helped identify vulnerable and intimidated witnesses for this survey. The Witness Service supplied details of all witnesses who they identified as vulnerable or intimidated to BMRB, an independent research company. Interviews for witnesses aged 13 or under were conducted with a parent or guardian answering on their behalf. Proxy interviews were also conducted with some other witnesses such as people with severe learning disabilities.

In phase 2, VIWs were similarly recruited at the same courts contacted in phase 1. A total of 552 witnesses were interviewed in phase 1 (a net response rate of 80%) and 569 in phase 2 (81%).

Main findings

Profile of VIWs

Of the 569 VIWs interviewed in phase 2, 42 per cent were aged under 17, 13 per cent reported a disability which limited daily activities, 70 per cent reported either fearing or experiencing intimidation, and 15 per cent were victims of a sexual offence. The overall profile of VIWs was reasonably similar to that found in phase 1, although the phase 2 survey included a higher proportion of child witnesses, witnesses actually experiencing intimidation, and VIWs based at magistrates' courts.

Witnesses affected by intimidation

The majority of VIWs in both phases of the research were affected by intimidation, either through direct experience (53% in phase 2) or because they feared intimidation (17% in phase 2). Intimidation was most likely to occur before the case reached court, but was also common while witnesses waited to give evidence. The survey findings uncovered a number of areas where intimidated witnesses were more satisfied in phase 2 than in phase 1 with their experience either before court or while at court.

For example, phase 2 witnesses were less likely to feel intimidated whilst waiting to give evidence (38% compared with 49% in phase 1) or whilst actually giving it (20% compared with 30%). The proportion of witnesses affected by intimidation in some way who felt that the police did not take action to prevent the intimidation fell from 45 per cent to 32 per cent. In addition, witnesses experiencing intimidation were more likely to consider that the intimidation had been dealt with effectively by the police where the police had been made aware of the problem (from 25% to 35%).

Although intimidated witnesses were more likely than average to be dissatisfied with their overall experience as a witness, it would appear that the above improvements in the experiences of intimidated witnesses have been reflected in improved satisfaction ratings. Among witnesses experiencing intimidation, overall satisfaction has increased from 48 per cent to 59 per cent and among those fearing intimidation, satisfaction has increased from 66 per cent to 80 per cent.

Satisfaction with aspects of the CJS

Compared with the Witness Satisfaction Survey (WSS) 2002 which covers all witnesses, VIWs were less satisfied with their overall experience. Overall 69 per cent were very or fairly satisfied with their treatment compared with 78 per cent in the WSS 2002 (Angle, Malam and Carey, 2003). This represents an improvement on the satisfaction rating among VIWs in phase 1. The increase from 64 per cent to 69 per cent is statistically significant at the 10 per cent level. Moreover there has been a significant decline in the proportion of VIWs very dissatisfied with their experience (from 22% in phase 1 to 17% in phase 2). The increase in overall satisfaction between phase 1 and 2 surveys was evident in most subgroups of witness vulnerability.

As in the WSS 2002, satisfaction was higher with individual criminal justice agencies than with the CJS overall. It was particularly high for the Witness Service, court staff and judges/magistrates.

Satisfaction ratings for individual agencies were largely unchanged between survey phases, with the exception of the defence lawyer where satisfaction fell from 45 per cent to 34 per cent. This was backed up by findings that prosecution witnesses in phase 2 were more likely than in phase 1 to consider that the defence lawyer lacked courtesy towards them and did not give them adequate opportunity to ask questions.

Satisfaction also varied by type of vulnerability. For example child witnesses (those aged under 17) tended to be more satisfied than adults (76% satisfied overall compared with 64% in phase 2), and people who had experienced or feared intimidation tended to be less satisfied than those who had not (64% compared to 81% in phase 2).

In both surveys, witnesses' satisfaction was particularly associated with intimidation, the verdict, satisfaction with court facilities and how much information they received. Multivariate analysis indicated that feeling satisfied with the police, feeling satisfied with the defence lawyer, feeling able to give their evidence accurately, and lack of feelings of anxiety or distress were all key drivers in explaining VIWs' overall satisfaction.

Although only 44 per cent of witnesses in phase 2 (no change from phase 1) said that they would be happy to be a witness again, a majority (61%) said that they would be a witness again if asked.

Anxiety

Most VIWs found being a witness stressful, although the level experiencing anxiety at any stage has declined between the two phases of the research from 77 per cent to 70 per cent. More specifically the proportion of VIWs experiencing anxiety at court reduced from 27 per cent to 17 per cent, and this reduction was reflected in all categories of witness vulnerabilities. Some aspects of their experience were clearly more distressing than others. The most commonly reported source of anxiety at both survey phases was seeing the defendant or their associates. Cross-examination was also very stressful, with 71 per cent of VIWs in phase 2 (no change from phase 1) saying that they found this "upsetting".

Special measures and other measures to assist VIWs

The phase 2 survey was conducted after the implementation of many of the special measures, while the phase 1 survey took place while only a limited number of such measures was in place, and these were only available for certain groups, in particular child witnesses. The results from the two surveys show an increase in the proportion of witnesses using certain measures, and the vast majority of witnesses using these measures in phase 2 found them helpful.

The largest increases in use of special measures were found among: video-recorded evidence-in-chief (from 30% to 42% among child witnesses); live television link for giving evidence (doubling from 43% to 83% among child witnesses); and removal of wigs and gowns (from 8% to 15% among Crown Court witnesses giving evidence).

Other forms of assistance including pagers, escorts and intermediaries[2] were used only rarely among VIWs at both stages (in the case of pagers, not at all).

Witnesses using special measures in phase 2 rated them very highly; for example nine in ten witnesses using the live TV link found this helpful, and a similar proportion found using video-recorded evidence-in-chief useful. The importance of special measures is further vindicated by the finding that 33 per cent of witnesses using any special measure said that they would not have been willing and able to give evidence without this.

---

2   It should be noted, however, that this special measure has yet to be formally implemented. (A date for implementation has yet to be decided.)

The value of special measures is further highlighted by the extensive level of demand for measures among witnesses who were not given access to them. Screens and/or live TV link were thought to be particularly useful, with around three-fifths of all VIWs who gave evidence and did not use these measures stating that they would have found them useful. VIWs also supported the idea of pagers or mobile phones, with 64 per cent saying that this would have been useful.

Consultation about measures

The 1999 Act creates a requirement on the court to consider the views of VIWs in decisions about special measures and other forms of assistance. The need to consult VIWs is also emphasised in guidance aimed at all criminal justice agencies (Home Office, 2000). Only 12 per cent of witnesses in the phase 1 survey said they were consulted about the use of measures, although this rose three-fold to 32 per cent in phase 2. In phase 2, nine in ten witnesses who were consulted about measures said that their views had been acted upon – at least to some extent.

Use of special measures and perceptions of the CJS

There were a number of areas where phase 2 witnesses using special measures displayed a heightened satisfaction with their experience when compared with witnesses not using such measures. In phase 2, it was found that witnesses using special measures were more likely to be satisfied overall compared with witnesses not using such measures (76% compared with 65%). There were also some more specific areas where there was evidence that witnesses using these measures were happier with their experience at court.

For example, witnesses using special measures were less likely than those not using them to experience anxiety (63% compared with 73%). Use of special measures was also associated with the impact of cross-examination, with 41 per cent of those using measures saying they had been upset a lot compared with 56 per cent not using measures (not significant). Witnesses using special measures were also more likely to have a favourable opinion of the CJS; for example they were more likely to believe that the CJS was effective in bringing criminals to justice, meets the needs of victims, and treats witnesses fairly and with respect.

Conclusions and recommendations

The results of the two surveys have demonstrated that efforts to improve the service received by VIWs have been reflected in enhanced satisfaction ratings. The increase in overall satisfaction from 64 per cent to 69 per cent is statistically significant at the 10 per cent level. Furthermore, the surveys have shown that the CJS appears to be taking more effective action against either real or feared intimidation, and that anxiety levels are reduced. Moreover, satisfaction as measured by a number of indicators has increased among most categories of vulnerability, although improved satisfaction is particularly evidence among witnesses affected by intimidation.

As expected, there has been increased use of special measures between the two phases of the research, particularly for measures which help avoid the need for the VIW to have to confront the defendant. When measures were used, they were valued very highly. Consultation about measures to assist VIWs has also increased significantly, although a majority (68%) are apparently still not consulted.

The survey results suggest that while satisfaction has improved in a number of areas, there is still some way to go before the needs of VIWs are fully met. Although reduced, anxiety levels among VIWs are still high. Additionally there is a still a fairly wide gap between the satisfaction ratings of VIWs and witnesses in general. However the provisions of the 1999 Act are not yet fully implemented, and it can be assumed that more widespread availability of special measures, including special measures not yet introduced such as video-recorded cross- or re-examination, will improve satisfaction further. Certainly the surveys show that there is more demand for use of measures.

Given the positive views of VIWs about the value of the various special measures, it would be expected that widespread implementation – alongside other initiatives to increase witness satisfaction generally – will raise satisfaction levels amongst vulnerable witnesses. These surveys have provided important evidence that the measures are working and will hopefully help drive even better service provision for this important group in the future.

This chapter sets out the background to the research, the research objectives and explains how the surveys were conducted. It then examines the characteristics of the vulnerable and intimidated witnesses (VIWs) who took part in the survey: demographics; the type of victim or witness; the type of case; and the categories of vulnerability. Where relevant, comparisons are made with the profile of all VIWs for whom recruitment forms were completed.

Background

The current government made a commitment to provide greater support and assistance for victims in rape and sexual offence trials and for VIWs generally.

> "This commitment arose from concerns that while measures are in place to assist child witnesses, many adult victims and witnesses find the criminal justice process daunting and stressful, particularly those who are vulnerable because of personal circumstances, including their relationship to the defendant or because of the nature of certain serious crimes, such as rape. Some witnesses are not always regarded as capable of giving evidence and so can be denied access to justice. Others are in fear of intimidation, which can result in either a failure to report offences in the first instance, or a refusal to give evidence in court."
>
> (Speaking Up For Justice, Home Office, 1998, p.1.)

To take forward the Government's commitment to this area, an interdepartmental working group was set up to undertake a wide-ranging review in 1997. *Speaking up for Justice* (Home Office, 1998) is the report of the interdepartmental working group on the treatment of VIWs in the criminal justice system (CJS). The report made 78 recommendations to improve the treatment of VIWs within the CJS and to enable them to give best evidence (i.e., evidence that is complete, coherent and accurate) in criminal proceedings. Special measures that required legislation were included in the Youth Justice and Criminal Evidence Act 1999. Other forms of assistance required administrative action and training. These measures cover the investigation stage, pre-trial support, the trial and beyond. Note that in this report, 'measures' is the global term that will be used to refer collectively to special measures and others forms of assistance for VIWs, whenever it is necessary to refer collectively to both.

Chapter I of Part II of the Youth Justice and Criminal Evidence Act 1999 Act contains a range of special measures to assist VIWs to give evidence in court. They are:

- *screens* – to ensure that the witness does not see the defendant;

- *video-recorded evidence-in-chief* – allowing an interview with the witness, which has been video-recorded before the trial, to be shown as the witness's evidence-in-chief in court;

- *live television link* – live television link or other arrangement allowing a witness to give evidence from outside the courtroom;

- *clearing the public gallery of the court* – so that evidence can be given in private;

- *removal of wigs and gowns in court;*

- *allowing the witness to use communication aids* – e.g., alphabet board (vulnerable witnesses only);

- *video-recorded pre-trial cross-examination and re-examination* – allowing a witness to be cross-examined or re-examined before the trial about their evidence, and a video recording of that cross-examination or re-examination to be shown at trial instead of the witness being cross-examined or re-examined live at trial; and

- *intermediaries* – allowing an approved intermediary to help a witness communicate with legal representatives and the court (vulnerable witnesses only).

In addition, other forms of assistance include:

- pre-court familiarisation visits;

- presence of a supporter in court;

- escorts to and from court;

- liaison officers;

- separate waiting areas; and

- use of pagers.

The categories of persons eligible for special measures are: children under the age of 17 at the time of the hearing; those who suffer from a mental or physical disorder, or who have a disability or impairment that is likely to affect their evidence; and those whose evidence is likely to be affected because of their fear or distress at giving evidence in the proceedings. Courts will determine whether a witness falls into any of these categories, although witnesses who are alleged to be victims of a sexual offence will be considered to be eligible for help with giving evidence unless they tell the court that they do not want to be considered eligible. Courts must also determine whether making particular measures available to an eligible witness will be likely to improve the quality of the evidence given by the witness and whether it might inhibit the testing of his/her evidence. However, for child witnesses in need of special protection (defined by section 21 of the 1999 Act) the provision of video-recorded evidence-in-chief or live television links is now the norm and it is not necessary to demonstrate that the use of these special measures would improve the quality of the witness's evidence.

Prosecution and defence witnesses who meet the criteria will be able to apply for special measures but defendants will not be eligible.

The majority of special measure set out in the 1999 Act were introduced in Crown Courts on 24 July 2002. All the special measures except pre-trial video-recorded cross-examination and re-examination and examination through an intermediary, which are the subject of separate pilot projects, have been implemented in the Crown Court for vulnerable witnesses. With the exception of video-recorded evidence-in-chief, the same special measures are available to intimidated witnesses in the Crown Court. Implementation in the magistrates' courts in July 2002 was restricted to the use of live television links and video-recorded evidence-in-chief for child witnesses in need of special protection. A wider range of measures are expected to be rolled out in 2004/05.

Therefore only the first six special measures listed above were included in the current evaluation. (The remaining two special measures will be evaluated separately at a later stage.)

Aims and objectives

Given the major significance of these changes, it was considered essential to assess their impact. The Home Office therefore commissioned research, the aims of which were:

1. to evaluate how well the special measures have been implemented throughout the CJS; and

2. to examine the experience of VIWs before and after the implementation of special measures in Crown Courts.

The present report deals with the second of these aims and reports on the findings of surveys of VIWs before and after implementation of the measures. The specific objectives of the survey of VIWs were:

1. to determine whether the introduction of the measures has been accompanied by an increase in VIWs' satisfaction within the CJS;

2. to determine to what extent the provision of support for VIWs has changed in practice with the implementation of special measures; and

3. to explore VIWs' attitudes to the measures.

The survey of VIWs was conducted in two phases. The purpose of the phase 1 survey was to collect baseline data before many of the special measures were implemented. This survey was conducted during the period November 2000 to February 2001 (see Kitchen and Elliott, 2001 for a summary of the main findings from phase 1). The phase 2 survey was conducted in the period April to June 2003, after the start of the implementation of special measures in Court Courts (which started in July 2002).

Methods

Phase 1 survey

All courts where there was a Witness Service[3] operating at the time of the phase 1 survey (86 Crown Courts, and 94 magistrates' courts) were asked if they would be

---

3   The Witness Service is run by Victim Support. Trained volunteers supported by Witness Service staff deliver the service. Since April 2002 the Witness Service is based in all Crown Courts and magistrates' courts in England and Wales.

willing to recruit witnesses for the survey. For the phase 1 survey, recruitment took place between October and December 2000. Witness Service-trained volunteers in these courts completed recruitment forms and returned details of all witnesses who they identified as being vulnerable or intimidated to BMRB. For the phase 1 survey, 62 Crown Courts and 48 magistrates' courts returned recruitment forms. In total, forms were returned for 1,234 witnesses, of whom 806 had agreed to be recontacted about the survey. Once ineligible and incomplete addresses were removed, 785 contacts were issued for fieldwork.

The phase 1 survey was developed by BMRB, in consultation with the Home Office and members of the VIW evaluation steering group, which included (among others) representatives from Victim Support[4] (VS), the Court Service, the Crown Prosecution Service (CPS), and Department of Health and the Association of Chief Police Officers (ACPO). The interview was piloted prior to main stage fieldwork. The average interview length was 42 minutes[5]. Before fieldwork began, a team comprising a BMRB researcher and a Home Office representative from the Research, Development and Statistics Directorate (RDS) conducted briefing sessions for the Witness Service at locations across England. The interviewers were also similarly briefed.

The fieldwork for the phase 1 survey took place between November 2000 and February 2001. Interviews were conducted face to face in witnesses' homes, using CAPI (Computer Assisted Personal Interviewing). All interviews where the witness was aged 13 or under were conducted with a parent or guardian answering on their behalf. Proxy interviews were also permitted in other situations where this was felt to be appropriate, for example, with slightly older witnesses whose parents felt they were too traumatised to take part, or witnesses with severe learning disabilities.

Most interviews were conducted with the witnesses themselves (88%) while 12 per cent were conducted with a parent or guardian answering on the witness's behalf. Proxy interviews were common when the witness was aged under 17, with 33 per cent of interviews being conducted with the parent or guardian of the witness. Three interviews with a witness aged between 17 and 24 years and one with a witness aged between 25 and 34 years were conducted with a parent or guardian. Two of these cases related to a sexual offence.

4   Victim Support (VS) is an independent charity receiving government financial support. VS volunteers offer emotional support, practical help and information to victims of crime and their families once a crime has taken place, as well as providing information about other organisations which may be able to help with specific problems. Victims can access the service whether or not the crime has been reported; many are referred by the police when they do report a crime.
5   A copy of the interview schedule can be obtained from the Home Office on request.

Before beginning the interview, BMRB interviewers were asked to check whether the final verdict had been reached on the case; this is because it was not felt to have been appropriate to interview witnesses while the case was still being heard. Witness Service volunteers were asked to estimate the final hearing date and BMRB telephoned several courts to check whether cases had been completed if there was doubt. However, of the 785 contacts issued to fieldwork, in 81 cases the witness was ineligible because the case had not been completed. A further 17 were ineligible for other reasons (mainly because they had moved or the address was untraceable). A total of 552 interviews were conducted which, once the ineligible addresses had been removed, represents a net response rate of 80 per cent. The gross response rate was 70 per cent.

Phase 2

The methods employed in phase 2 were very similar to those in phase 1 in order to maintain comparability between the surveys. A decision was made to recruit witnesses for phase 2 in the same courts selected for phase 1 – this included courts which did not return any forms in phase 1. The Witness Service was similarly briefed at four locations across England, and recruitment took place between March and May 2003.

Of the 86 Crown Courts and 94 magistrates' courts contacted, 71 Crown Courts and 67 magistrates' courts returned recruitment forms. This represents a higher return rate compared with phase 1[6]. In total, forms were returned for 2,050 witnesses, of whom 1,229 had agreed to be recontacted about the survey. Once ineligible and incomplete addresses were removed, 793 contacts were issued for fieldwork. The total number of interviews achieved was 569 which, after removing 55 cases where contact was not attempted by an interviewer and 38 ineligible cases, represented a net response rate of 81 per cent. The level of interviews conducted by proxy (i.e., with parent or guardian of the witness) was similar to phase 1 with 14 per cent being conducted in this way (30% for child witnesses).

Although most questions remained the same, the phase 2 survey was revised in places; this mainly occurred due to the addition of more questions on measures for VIWs. Where question wording changed in a way that could have affected comparability, this is detailed in the narrative text. The interview length at phase 2 was slightly longer than at phase 1: 50 minutes.

---

6   As explained in more detail in Appendix A, the higher level of involvement in phase 2 may be explained by a number of factors, including a more efficient and better-staffed Witness Service (some had only just been set up at the time of the phase 1 survey) and VIWs being easier to identify. We also sought to include more WS co-ordinators in the initial briefings at phase 2.

A more detailed description of the survey procedures, including response rates can be found in Appendix A.

Note on interpretation of survey data

All data reported in this volume are unweighted[7]. Given the lack of other information on the number of VIWs, it is not clear whether the sample reflected the wider population of VIWs. It should be noted that some vulnerabilities are easier to identify than others, for example. it is often easier to identify child witnesses than witnesses with learning disabilities. It is therefore possible that the sample was skewed towards those easier to identify and therefore was not wholly representative of the wider population of VIWs. However, the profile of those interviewed closely matched that of all witnesses approached, indicating that there was not a significant response bias. Further details of these profiles can be found in Appendix A.

Figures are reported from a base excluding those who gave a 'don't know' response. For questions where the 'don't know' response accounted for more than five per cent of responses, this is indicated and included in the base. Where comparisons between statistics have been drawn (either between subgroups in one of the surveys or between the two surveys) differences are statistically significant at the 95 per cent confidence level, unless otherwise indicated.

Characteristics of VIWs interviewed

Demographic profile

Demographic information about VIWs was collected at the end of the interview, including age, sex, geographical region, ethnic background and social grade. Data on the demographic profile of the two survey samples is shown in Table 1.1.

Of the 552 VIWs interviewed in the phase 1 survey, 57 per cent were female and 43 per cent were male. The proportions were similar in phase 2 (60% female, 40% male). This probably reflects the fact that victims of sexual offences are often perceived as vulnerable and that many such victims are female.

As witnesses aged under 17 were one of the target groups recruited, and are more easily identifiable than some other vulnerable witnesses, it is understandable that they made up a

---

7   "Unweighted" means that the data have not been adjusted to match population statistics of the profile of VIWs as these were not available. Where it is considered that certain subgroups of VIWs may have been over- or under-represented, this is discussed in later sections of this chapter and (in more detail) in Appendix A.

significant majority of all VIWs taking part in the surveys. In phase 1, 34 per cent of the VIWs interviewed were aged under 17 at the time of the hearing, although this rose to 42 per cent in phase 2.

Most VIWs who were interviewed described themselves as white (90% in phase 2), with only a small proportion describing themselves as black (3%), Asian (3%) or other (4%)[8]. This is similar to the ethnic breakdown of the phase 1 survey.

The geographical regions with the largest proportions of VIWs interviewed were (in phase 2) the North with 35 per cent, and the Midlands with 31 per cent of VIWs. A quarter (24%) lived in the South East, while one in ten (10%) lived in the South West or Wales. The regional distribution in phase 2 differs from that in phase 1, mainly in the respect that a higher proportion of interviews in phase 1 were conducted in the South West and Wales.

The social grade of VIWs was derived from questions asked at the end of the interview about household income and the working status of the chief income earner in the household. While only eight per cent in phase 2 belonged to the wealthier social groups of AB (which covers higher and intermediate managerial, administrative and professional groups), the sample was otherwise spread fairly evenly across the different groups. About half (46%) were in groups C1 or C2 (the junior managerial, administrative and professional group and skilled manual group) and a similar proportion (47%) were in groups D (semi-skilled and unskilled manual) or E (state dependants, casual and lowest grade workers). This was similar to the social grade profile in phase 1.

Type of court

In phase 1, 62 per cent of VIWs were witnesses to a case being heard at Crown Court, and 38 per cent at magistrates' courts. At phase 2, the representation of magistrates' court witnesses increased significantly to 57 per cent of VIWs interviewed, with Crown Court witnesses accounting for only 43 per cent. This is accounted for by the fact that (as detailed earlier) a higher proportion of the magistrates' courts approached actually recruited a sample for the survey in phase 2 (67 out of 94) compared with phase 1 (48 out of 94), coupled with a much lower increase in the proportion of Crown Courts getting involved. There could be a number of reasons for this. It was known that some magistrates' courts approached did not recruit any sample for phase 1 either because no vulnerable witnesses were identified over the recruitment period or because the Witness

---

8   Witnesses were shown a card listing 15 ethnic groups and asked to say which they identified with, but the groups have been aggregated here because of the low numbers who identified themselves as a member of a minority ethnic group.

Service was not up and running or was understaffed (see Appendix A). It seems reasonable to assume that by phase 2 these magistrates' courts may have had a more efficiently run Witness Service, and/or that more VIWs would have been identified due to the improved processes to identify such witnesses in advance.

Table 1.1:   Demographic profile of VIW samples

Base: All VIWs	Phase 1 (n=552)	Phase 2 (n=569)
	%	%
Gender		
Male	43	40
Female	57	60
Age at time of hearing		
Aged under 17	34	42
Aged 17+	66	58
Social grade		
AB	11	8
C1	26	22
C2	23	23
DE	41	47
Ethnicity		
White	89	90
Non-white or mixed	11	10
Region		
North	28	35
Midlands	31	31
South East	20	24
South West/Wales	21	10

Contact with the criminal justice system

A quarter of VIWs interviewed (24% phase 1, 26% phase 2) had some previous experience or knowledge of the criminal justice system. Most commonly this had been gained by previously acting as a witness (11% in phase 2). A small proportion (7%) had previously appeared in court as a defendant, while two per cent had acted as a juror. Nine per cent of VIWs in the phase 2 survey said they had prior knowledge of courts gained in some other way.

Type of witness

Most VIWs taking part in the survey were prosecution witnesses: in phase 2, 62 per cent were the victims of an offence, while 37 per cent were other witnesses for the prosecution. These proportions are unchanged from phase 1 (58% victims, 41% other prosecution witnesses). A very small proportion of VIWs (2% phase 1, 1% phase 2) were defence witnesses. The low proportion of defence witnesses in this survey reflects the greater reliance on the Witness Service to recruit the sample, who tend to have very little contact with defence witnesses. This is because referral is mostly from the CPS; defence lawyers are generally not so good at referring defence witnesses to the Witness Service. However, it also seems plausible that fewer defence witnesses are vulnerable. Defence lawyers may have more choice about who to call as defence witnesses. They may call many as character witnesses, and might be expected to avoid selecting vulnerable witnesses. In contrast, prosecution lawyers may have little choice about whether to call a vulnerable witness to give evidence where that person is the victim of the crime. In both phases, the profile of all witnesses approached at the recruitment stage was very similar to the group who were interviewed (see Appendix A).

Type of offence

The most common offences in the case the witness was involved with are shown in Figure 1.1.

Violent and sexual offences were most common: similarly to phase 1, 49 per cent of VIWs in phase 2 were witnesses for violence against the person cases, and 22 per cent were witnesses for sexual offence cases.

This offence profile also helps explain the greater representation of women in this survey. Women were much more likely than men to be witnesses in sexual offence cases (in phase 2 29% of women, compared with just 10% of men), while men were more likely to be witnesses in serious violence cases (18% of men, compared with 9% of women). The offence profile also helped explain the age profile of the respondents. Those aged between17 and 24 were the age group most likely to be involved in sexual offence cases (31%), while 25-34 year olds were the most likely to be witnesses in serious violence cases (22%).

Figure 1.1: Offence type[9]

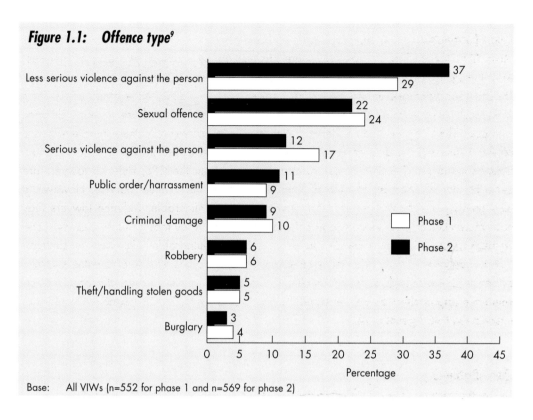

Base: All VIWs (n=552 for phase 1 and n=569 for phase 2)

Category of vulnerability

Figure 1.2 shows the categories of vulnerability of witnesses taking part in the survey, according to their own definitions in the interview. Individual categories of vulnerability are discussed further in the following sections. Note that witnesses may be vulnerable in more than one way (see further below).

---

9   Interviewers had available a classification card to help witnesses classify offences. "Serious violence against the person" included murder, attempted murder, manslaughter, wounding/causing grievous bodily harm (GBH), causing death by reckless/dangerous driving. "Less serious violence" included assault causing actual bodily harm (ABH), (common) assault, assault on a police constable, cruelty to or neglect of children, threats or conspiracy to kill.

Figure 1.2: *Categories of vulnerability (self-defined)*

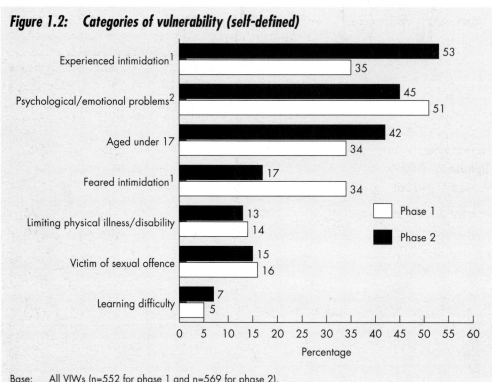

Base: All VIWs (n=552 for phase 1 and n=569 for phase 2).
1 Readers should note that VIWs' self-defined categorisation of experience and fear of intimidation does not necessarily concord with the legal definition – see later in this chapter for further discussion on this.
2 Psychological problems alone are not recognised as a category of vulnerability. However, many VIWs did experience problems of this nature; this is discussed later in this chapter.

Table 1.2 shows that there was a large amount of overlap between some categories of vulnerability. For example, 66 per cent of witnesses with a limiting disability or illness reported experiencing intimidation at the time of being a witness, and 58 per cent of victims of a sexual offence also reported psychological or emotional problems.

Table 1.2: **Percentage overlap between different categories of vulnerability in phase 2 (equivalent phase 1 figures shown in brackets)[10]**

	Aged under 17	Victim of sexual offence	Limiting physical disability/illness	Psychological problems	Experienced intimidation
Proportion of those aged under 17 (phase 2: n=239, phase 1: n=186)	100	15 (25)	3 (4)	28 (38)	46 (28)
Proportion of victims of sexual offence (phase 2: n=84, phase 1: n=89)	42 (52)	100	12 (7)	58 (69)	45 (34)
Proportion of witnesses with limiting physical disability or illness (phase 2: n=74, phase 1: n=77)	9 (9)	14 (8)	100 (71)	73	66 (39)
Proportion of witnesses with psychological problems (phase 2: n=256, phase 1: n=280)	26 (25)	19 (22)	21 (20)	100	65 (40)
Proportion of witnesses who experienced intimidation (phase 2: n=304, phase 1: n=192)	36 (27)	13 (16)	16 (16)	55 (58)	100

The number of vulnerabilities each person possessed was also examined. The following were counted[10]:

---

10 Psychological problems alone are not recognised as a category of vulnerability (and VIWs were not recruited on the basis of this), although Table 1.2 shows that there is a significant overlap between these types of problem and other recognised categories of vulnerability. In addition the count of vulnerabilities also includes membership of an ethnic minority group and language difficulties, which are also not recognised categories of vulnerability, although arguably they are important factors in relation to VIWs' well-being in court.

- child (aged under 17);
- victim of sexual offence;
- experienced intimidation;
- reports a disability or illness (excluding those reported as having a learning disability);
- reports a learning disability;
- member of a minority ethnic group; and
- difficulties with English (both as a first or second language).

Table 1.3: Number of vulnerabilities

Base: All VIWs	Phase 1 (n=552) %	Phase 2 (n=569) %
1	35	43
2	29	31
3	19	9
More than three	7	3
No vulnerabilities	11	13

On this basis, as shown in Table 1.3, 43 per cent in phase 2 could be classed as having one vulnerability, 31 per cent as having two, nine per cent as having three, and three per cent as having more than three vulnerabilities. Compared with phase 1, there has been a fall in the proportion of witnesses with three or more vulnerabilities and an increase in the proportion with only one vulnerability.

Around one in eight (11% phase 1, 13% phase 2) were not counted as having any of these vulnerabilities. However, if feared intimidation was included, the proportion not counted as having any vulnerabilities fell to only five and eight per cent respectively. The existence of a group that apparently possessed no vulnerabilities may be partly explained by the fact that the study did not examine the relationship of the witness to the defendant, and some might actually have been vulnerable because they knew the defendant. In some cases, sexual orientation may have been relevant. Respondents were not asked about this because it was felt this was too intrusive.

Witnesses with disability or illness

Figure 1.2 shows that 13 per cent of VIWs in phase 2 said that they had a disability or long-term illness that limited their everyday activities at the time they were a witness. This compares with nine per cent who were identified at the recruitment stage, possibly indicating that witnesses were more willing to disclose disability or illness in the context of an interview by an independent researcher.

Witnesses with psychological/emotional problems

Although psychological problems alone are not recognised as a category of vulnerability under the 1999 Act, a large proportion of VIWs (45% at phase 2) said that they had some form of psychological or emotional problem at the time of being a witness. Women were more likely than men to report some kind of problem (49% compared with 39%) and the likelihood of experiencing such problems appeared to increase according to the age of the witness: 28 per cent of witnesses aged under 17 reported problems, rising to 56 per cent of those aged between 17 and 34 and 55 per cent of those aged 35 and over.

A wide range of psychological and emotional problems were cited by those witnesses in phase 2 reporting such problems, including stress (34%) 'nerves' or anxiety (mentioned by 27%), depression (18%) difficulty sleeping (15%), being overly emotional (13%), and fear of going out (9%).

Witnesses with difficulties reading and writing English

VIWs were asked whether they had any difficulties reading and writing English and similarly to the phase 1 survey, seven per cent reported such difficulties.

Intimidated witnesses

In the interview, witnesses were asked about intimidation, including fear of threats, by someone in connection with the case (excluding lawyers or court personnel). Fears of intimidation are important as they may give some indication of community-wide intimidation, in which a general climate of fear and non-cooperation with the criminal justice system is created amongst a community. This may be contrasted with case specific intimidation, in which intimidation is targeted against particular individuals. The term 'intimidation' was not defined for respondents and may therefore cover a fairly broad range of experiences, including verbal threats and physical harassment, or fears related to general signs of urban decay and anti-social behaviour within a particular area. The legal definition is much narrower, focusing on threats or acts against a person, their property or a third party (such as a relative) which are intended to intimidate, with the intention of obstructing the course of justice[11].

The majority of VIWs interviewed felt they were affected by intimidation in some way (69% in phase 1, 70% in phase 2). However, between phases 1 and 2, there was an increase in the level of witnesses experiencing as opposed to just fearing intimidation (this is partly explained by a change in the question wording – see Chapter 2). In phase 2, over half (53%) of witnesses said that they had experienced intimidation in relation to the case, and a further one in six (17%) said they had feared intimidation but not actually experienced any. This was in contrast to the phase 1 survey where proportions experiencing and only fearing intimidation was more balanced (35% and 34% respectively).

In both phases, there was quite a large discrepancy between the proportion of intimidated witnesses identified at the recruitment stage and the proportion identified at the interview stage, with more intimidated witnesses being identified in the latter. In phase 1, 44 per cent of all witnesses approached were said to have feared or experienced intimidation, against 69 per cent admitting this in the interview. In phase 2 the equivalent figures were 54 per cent (recruitment stage) and 70 per cent (interview stage). However, this is likely to be attributable to the different ways in which such data was collected at these stages. At the recruitment stage, Witness Service volunteers asked witnesses whether they had "either feared or experienced any threats or intimidation since the original offence?". In the survey, a more detailed set of questions was asked to elicit experience or fear of intimidation. Thus, this suggests that the Witness Service was not aware of all cases where the witnesses feared or experienced intimidation.

The high percentage fearing or experiencing intimidation may also reflect a different understanding among witnesses of what intimidation means compared with criminal justice practitioners. It seems plausible, for example, that witnesses might associate general worries about giving evidence with intimidation. Attempts were made to avoid this in the interview by explicitly stating that these concerns should only be included if they stemmed from fears that someone else involved in the case might intimidate them. At the phase 2 survey a new question was added to probe for the reasons why witnesses were made to feel intimidated or threatened. (See Chapter 2 for more detailed findings relating to witness intimidation.)

---

11 See Home Office 1998, Annex A , for a discussion of the types of intimidation and how they relate.

Structure of the report

The structure adopted throughout this report generally follows the same order as the criminal justice process. Chapter 2 considers VIWs' experiences before court, Chapter 3 experiences at court, and Chapter 4 examines the experience of giving evidence and cross-examination. Chapter 5 explores what happens after giving evidence. Chapter 6 looks at VIWs' experiences of those special measures available, and Chapter 7 examines VIWs' satisfaction with different aspects of the CJS and overall. Chapter 8 then draws some conclusions. Findings from both the pre-implementation survey (phase 1) and the post-implementation survey (phase 2) are presented and compared throughout the report.

Key points

- The majority of VIWs who took part in the surveys were prosecution witnesses – around two-thirds were victims of crime and around one-third were other prosecution witnesses. Only a very small proportion were defence witnesses.

- Around three-fifths of VIWs interviewed were females, reflecting in part the inclusion of victims of sexual offences, most of whom were women. Around 40 per cent of VIWs in both surveys were male.

- In terms of self-defined vulnerability, the most frequently reported vulnerabilities were (in rank order for phase 2): experienced intimidation, experienced psychological/emotional problems, under 17 years, feared intimidation, victim of a sexual offence and limited physical illness/disability.

- Over two-thirds of witnesses reported being affected by intimidation – the proportion experiencing intimidation as opposed to fearing it increased between phase 1 and phase 2.

---

2   **Experiences before court**

This chapter examines VIWs' experiences of the CJS before attending court. It explores intimidation and sources of information, contact with the police, and support before court.

Intimidation

Who was affected by intimidation

All VIWs were asked whether there was any point at which they experienced or feared intimidation. The term "intimidation" was explained as being scared or threatened by anyone involved in the case such as the defendant, victim, another witness, or friends and family of these people (but excluding lawyers or other court personnel).

Experience of intimidation was very prevalent in both phases of the research among the VIWs interviewed. In phase 1, 69 per cent said that they either feared or experienced intimidation, with 34 per cent fearing it and 35 per cent actually experiencing it. In phase 2, the overall level of intimidation was very similar with 70 per cent being affected by intimidation. However, the proportion of those experiencing as opposed to simply fearing it has increased with 53 per cent saying that they had actually experienced intimidation, and 17 per cent fearing it[12].

The nature of intimidation either feared or experienced is covered in more detail in a later section (see Table 2.1). However, it should be noted at this stage that not all respondents who said that they experienced or feared intimidation actually suffered direct threats or actions. Much of the reported experience or fear was related to a more general anxiety about the defendant or the defendant's associates.

As in phase 1, more victims in phase 2 said they experienced intimidation than other prosecution witnesses (59% compared with 44%), although there was little difference in the proportions saying they feared intimidation (16% compared to 19%). Slightly fewer child witnesses experienced intimidation (46%) compared with adult witnesses (59%). Experience of intimidation was slightly higher for those with a physical disability (65%) or who suffered psychological or emotional problems (also 65%).

---

12 This may in part be caused by a slightly different way in which the question was asked in the two surveys. In phase 1, witnesses were asked in one question about whether intimidation was experienced or feared, whereas in 2003, witnesses were asked about experience first, and then fear, in two separate questions.

When did intimidation occur

Figure 2.1 shows the points in the criminal justice process at which witnesses experienced or feared intimidation (witnesses may have mentioned more than one stage).

Figure 2.1: When witnesses felt intimidation

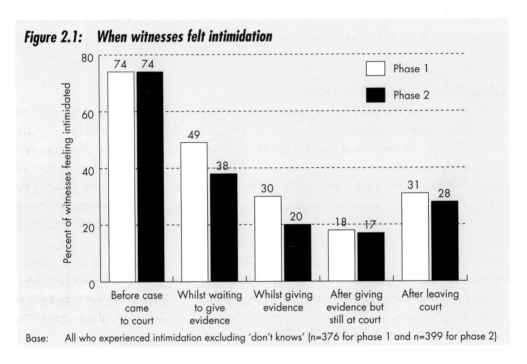

Base: All who experienced intimidation excluding 'don't knows' (n=376 for phase 1 and n=399 for phase 2)

The results of both surveys show that witnesses appear to be at greatest risk before attending court, with the risk falling throughout the process, but rising slightly again after leaving court. One explanation might be the presence of court staff, police and lawyers at court, which may reduce opportunities for intimidation. In phase 2, witnesses who actually experienced some form of intimidation were more likely than those who only feared it to say it happened either whilst waiting to give evidence (41% compared with 26%) or when they were actually giving evidence (23% compared with 11%). In phase 1, it was found that witnesses in Crown Court were more likely than those in magistrates' courts to feel intimidated whilst waiting to give evidence (54% compared with 41%), suggesting a relationship between intimidation and the seriousness of the case. However, in phase 2, the general pattern of when intimidation was felt or experienced was the same in both types of court.

When comparing the results of the survey pre- and post-implementation of special measures, it would appear that, while levels of intimidation were the same before court and after giving evidence, in the later research, witnesses were less likely to be affected by intimidation whilst waiting to give evidence (38% in phase 2 compared with 49% in phase 1), or whilst actually giving evidence (20% compared with 30%). This is a very encouraging result, and suggests that, while intimidation is still as prevalent in phase 2 compared with phase 1, measures targeted at reducing intimidation either inside the courtroom or whilst witnesses are waiting to give evidence, have been effective in reducing feelings of intimidation at these key stages (see Chapter 6 for more details).

Who was responsible for intimidation

Witnesses who felt intimidated were asked who had made them feel this way. This could be more than one person. The pattern of responses was very similar in phase 2 to that in phase 1. In phase 2, the defendant was by far the most likely person to make witnesses feel intimidated, with 68 per cent saying this was the case. The principal further sources of intimidation were friends and family of the defendant (44% of those who were affected by intimidation) and just a general feeling which they could not attribute to a particular person (14%). A small proportion (5%) mentioned feeling intimidated by a defence witness, while three per cent said that the defence lawyer intimidated them.

Those who actually experienced intimidation were far more likely than those who only feared it to cite a particular person, with 72 per cent in phase 2 attributing their experience to the defendant and 50 per cent to friends or family of the defendant (these figures for those fearing intimidation were respectively 58% and 23%).

Nature of intimidation

In phase 2, for the first time, witnesses affected by intimidation were asked to articulate in which ways they were made to feel intimidated or threatened. Witnesses gave responses in their own words which were later coded into the categories shown in Table 2.1.

Among those actually experiencing intimidation, the main source of intimidation was threats, either from the defendant directly (36%) or from the defendant's family or friends (21%). Nine per cent were scared of seeing the defendant in court, while eight per cent were scared of seeing the defendant either before or after the case. A small proportion (6%) mentioned actual violence by the defendant, while three per cent said that they had been offered money by the defendant or his or her associates to drop the case.

Fearing intimidation was mainly a result of fear that they would see the defendant outside of the courtroom (31%) or a more general fear of the defendant or his or her family/friends (21%).

Table 2.1: Why witnesses felt intimidated or threatened (phase 2)

Base: All fearing or experiencing intimidation	Total (n=400)	Feared intimidation (n=96)	Experienced intimidation (n=304)
	%	%	%
Threats by defendant	29	8	36
Threats by defendant's family	17	3	21
Scared of seeing defendant before/after case	14	31	8
General fear of defendant or his/her family/friends	11	21	7
Scared of seeing defendant in court	10	10	9
Scared of seeing defendant's family/friends before/after case	6	11	5
Violence by defendant	6	4	6
Violence by unknown person	3	-	4
Offered money by defendant or his/her family/friends to drop case	3	-	3

Reporting intimidation

Witnesses who felt intimidated were asked if they had reported this officially. In phase 2, 65 per cent of those who either feared or experienced intimidation said that they had done so, a slightly lower proportion than in phase 1 (69%)[13]. There is evidence that those who feared intimidation as opposed to actually experiencing it were less likely to report this in phase 2 when compared with phase 1 (36% compared with 61%). However, there was little difference in the rate of reporting for those experiencing intimidation (74% in phase 2, 78% in phase 1).

Witnesses were also asked who they reported this to (some gave more than one answer). Of those who reported intimidation, most reported to the police (83%), followed by the Witness Service (20%) and the CPS or lawyers (10%). There were no statistically significant differences on this measure when compared with phase 1.

Those witnesses who felt intimidated but did not report such feelings to the police were asked if the police were made aware, by some other means, of their feelings of intimidation. Including those cases where the witness did report feelings of intimidation, the police were known to be aware of about 62 per cent of cases (64% in phase 1), rising to

---

13 p>.05 not statistically significant.

70 per cent among those who experienced intimidation (73% in phase 1). Although this may seem high, it should be remembered that only witnesses whose cases reached court were included in the sample, so this may not be representative of all intimidated witnesses. It seems plausible that cases involving witnesses who did not report intimidation were less likely to reach court, as the intimidation may have 'successfully' dissuaded the witness from cooperating further with the CJS.

Action taken by the police against intimidation

As just noted, in phase 2, witnesses claimed that the police learned about 62 per cent of cases where they felt intimidated. In phase 1, 45 per cent of this subgroup said that the police did not take any action about the intimidation. In phase 2, however, this proportion had reduced to 32 per cent, suggesting that the police were now more effective in taking action against intimidation.

Actions taken by the police were very similar in phase 2 compared with phase 1. A range of actions had been employed but, according to intimidated witnesses who had been in contact with the police over this matter, the principal steps taken by the police in phase 2 were speaking to those responsible (22%) and arresting someone in connection with the intimidation (9%). Very small numbers of witnesses in this subgroup mentioned other types of action; for example five per cent said that the witness had been re-housed either temporarily or permanently, four per cent said that the police provided reassurance, three per cent said that the police took a statement from them and a further three per cent said that the police stayed with them. Some of these results appear low on the face of it. However, these results should be seen in the context of it being likely that witnesses for whom very serious actions had to be taken to prevent intimidation would have been less willing to be contacted for interview.

Whether police action stopped intimidation

All witnesses who said that the police took some form of action to stop them feeling intimidated were asked whether this action had actually stopped the intimidation. The proportion saying that the action taken by the police did not succeed in preventing them being intimidated fell slightly between phase 1 and phase 2 from 43 per cent to 38 per cent. Witnesses reported that police action succeeded in stopping intimidation in only 33 per cent per cent of cases (up from 25% in phase 1), with 29 per cent saying that it stopped to some extent (30% in phase 1)[14].

---

14 None of the differences between phase 1 and phase 2 reported in this paragraph are statistically significant.

How effectively intimidation before court was dealt with

Witnesses who felt intimidated before court and reported it were asked how effectively they felt the intimidation had been dealt with.

As shown in Table 2.2, only 33 per cent of witnesses in phase 1 who felt intimidated before court, in cases where the police knew about it, considered that the intimidation had been dealt with effectively. This proportion rose slightly to 39 per cent in phase 2. In phase 1, those who had feared but not actually experienced intimidation were more likely to feel that action had been effective, with 44 per cent saying it had been dealt with 'very' or 'quite' effectively, compared with 25 per cent of those who experienced intimidation. This may be because intimidation that witnesses feared was actually prevented or that witnesses felt reassured by the police. However, it is unclear exactly what action, beyond support and reassurance, the police could or should take when intimidation is merely feared rather than experienced.

A large proportion (54%) of those experiencing intimidation in phase 1 thought that it had been dealt with 'not at all effectively', although the equivalent proportion was slightly lower in phase 2 (45%). Overall, the proportion of witnesses experiencing intimidation, in cases where the police were made aware of the matter, who believed that the matter had been dealt with effectively rose from 25 per cent to 35 per cent[15]. This is a promising trend, although the results suggest that there is still some way to go before witnesses can be said to be fully satisfied that their concerns have been appropriately dealt with.

As in phase 1, those in phase 2 who considered that intimidation had not been dealt with effectively were more likely to have been dissatisfied with their experience as a witness (52%) compared with those who felt that the police had been effective in their action (24% dissatisfied).

---

15 None of the differences between the phase 1 and phase 2 data reported in this paragraph are statistically significant.

Table 2.2: **How effectively intimidation before court was dealt with**

	All who reported to police/ police came to hear		Experienced intimidation		Feared intimidation*
	Phase 1 (n=224) %	Phase 2 (n=230) %	Phase 1 (n=130) %	Phase 2 (n=196) %	Phase 1 (n=94) %
Very effectively	13	15	10	15	18
Quite effectively	20	24	15	20	26
Not very effectively	17	16	17	16	17
Not at all effectively	41	41	54	45	22
Don't know	9	4	4	4	17
Effectively	33	39	25	35	44
Not effectively	58	57	71	61	39

* Figures based on those fearing intimidation in phase 2 are not shown due to small base size

Action that should have been taken about intimidation before court

Witnesses who felt that the intimidation they feared or experienced before court had not been dealt with effectively were asked, unprompted, what they thought should have been done about it. The responses given by witnesses in phase 2 were similar to those given in phase 1. Stronger action to deal with those responsible for intimidation was requested by a number of witnesses in phase 2. A significant minority (20%) said that the police should have spoken to or issued a warning to the person responsible, while 11 per cent said that those responsible should have been arrested. Ten per cent said that the person responsible for making them feel intimidated should have been kept on remand until the case came to court, and a further ten per cent said that they thought the defendant should have been made to stay away from the area where the witness lived. The other main requirement was for witnesses' concerns about intimidation to be listened to, with five per cent saying that the police should have taken their concerns more seriously, and three per cent saying the police should have given them more reassurance.

Investigation stage

Contact with the police

In phase 2, nearly all VIWs (96%) said that they had had some form of contact with the police in relation to the case (98% in phase 1), and most of these had given a statement. Forty-two per cent of witnesses under the age of 17 in phase 2 made a videotaped statement compared with 30 per cent in phase 1[16]. A further 15 witnesses aged over 17 when called as a witness gave evidence via video in phase 2 (representing 14% of all VIWs giving videotaped evidence). Chapter 6 provides further details of video-recorded evidence-in-chief.

As in phase 1, nearly half (44%) of VIWs in phase 2 volunteered evidence to the police, while 31 per cent were asked by the police for help. In 25 per cent of cases, someone contacted the police on the witness's behalf. This was more likely to happen with younger witnesses, with 32 per cent of those aged below 17 saying this was the case.

Telephoning the police was the most common form of making initial contact in phase 2, with 56 per cent of all vulnerable witnesses, and 69 per cent of victims saying they had done this. Police visited the home of 15 per cent of VIWs as a first contact, although this was more likely to have happened for prosecution witnesses who were not victims of the incident (25%) than witnesses who were victims (10%). It was less common for VIWs to visit the police station in person (10%) and for the police to telephone the witness (7%). In a small proportion of cases (6%) first contact was made at the crime scene. There were no significant differences between these figures and the equivalent figures in the phase 1 survey.

All VIWs who had had any contact with the police were asked if they felt the police had treated them with courtesy. The vast majority of these VIWs felt the police had done so (92% both phases).

Giving a statement

In phase 2 as in phase 1, most VIWs (91%) said that they were told they were likely to be called as a witness when they gave their statement. Just three per cent were told it was unlikely they would be called, while five per cent were not told whether or not it was likely.

Most VIWs in phase 2 (67%) said they were allowed to have someone with them when they gave their statement; 18 per cent said this had not been allowed and a further 14 per cent said they did not need anyone with them. The vast majority of witnesses under the age of 17 were allowed to have someone with them when making their statement (86%). These results remain unchanged from phase 1.

---

16 It should be noted that this increase may be partly due to a change in question wording in 2003. In phase 1 children were asked simply whether they gave information to the police that was videotaped. In 2003, this question was elaborated by giving child witnesses (or their parents) an explanation. "The police sometimes videotape interviews with witnesses in advance, so that they do not have to stand up in court and give evidence, although they may still be cross-examined about it."

VIWs who gave a statement in phase 2 were asked if they had seen any specialist officers when giving their statements. Most VIWs (66%) said that they had not seen any specialist officer. However it should be noted that some VIWs may have seen a specialist officer and not identified his or her as such, or may have forgotten. Ten per cent of all those asked did not know whether or not they had seen a specialist officer. Victims of sexual offences (61%) were more likely to report having seen a specialist officer. These findings remain unchanged from phase 1.

Most VIWs (81% in phase 2, 82% in phase 1) felt the police had given them enough support when they gave their statement. This figure was particularly high among witnesses aged under 17 (88% in phase 2, 89% in phase 1). There was no significant difference according to sex or type of witness in either survey year. Witnesses with disabilities/illness were slightly more likely than average to say they had not been given enough support, and the difference in phase 2 was significant (27% compared with 18%). In phase 2, witnesses who had experienced intimidation were less likely to feel they were given enough support (76%) than witnesses who feared intimidation (86%) and those who neither feared nor experienced intimidation (90%).

In phase 2 as in phase 1, VIWs who said the police had given them enough support were more likely to feel satisfied with their overall experience (77% compared with 38% of those who did not feel they were given enough support). Similarly, 48 per cent of those who said they had received sufficient support when giving their statement said they would be happy to be a witness again, compared with only 24 per cent of those who felt they did not have sufficient support saying this. This indicates that support from the police at this initial stage is an important factor in overall satisfaction and willingness to be a witness again.

Police contact after statement was made

VIWs who made a statement were asked if the police had kept them informed about the progress of the case.

In phase 2, just over a third of VIWs said that they had not been kept informed at all about the progress of the case (36% compared with 38% in phase 1). A little over a quarter of VIWs said that they had been kept regularly informed, a slight reduction compared with phase 1 (32%)[17], while the remaining 37 per cent said that they had been informed occasionally (30% in phase 1).

---

17 Not statistically significant.

In phase 2 as in phase 1, VIWs involved in cases at the Crown Court were more likely to be kept regularly informed than those at magistrates' courts (33% compared with 23%), while over two-thirds (43%) of VIWs at magistrates' courts had not been informed at all about the progress of the case. As in phase 1, being kept regularly informed by police was strongly related to satisfaction. In phase 2, VIWs who had been kept regularly informed were more satisfied with their overall experience (85% compared with only 60% of those not kept informed).

Most VIWs (75%) recalled being given a number by the police that they could call with any queries relating to the case (no change since phase 1). Victims were slightly more likely than other prosecution witnesses to be given a telephone number (78% compared with 71%), and the vast majority (90%) of victims of sexual offences recalled being given a number.

Compared with phase 1, a smaller proportion of VIWs given a telephone number in phase 2 actually called it (53% compared with 62%). Subgroups most likely to call the telephone number provided to them in phase 2 were women (57% compared with 47% men), and witnesses who had experienced some form of intimidation (64% compared with 33% of those who neither feared nor experienced intimidation). VIWs in the Crown Court were also more likely to call the telephone number than those in the magistrates' courts (64% compared with 43%). Cases which go to Crown Court tend to be more serious and lengthy than those dealt with at magistrates' courts, and this may explain why Crown Court witnesses in particular needed to call to find out what was happening.

Most VIWs who called the telephone number found the police to be helpful (82% in phase 2, 78% in phase 1). The more detailed pattern of responses in phase 2 was similar to that in phase 1, with 48 per cent saying they were 'very helpful', 34 per cent 'quite helpful' and 18 per cent did not find the police helpful when they called.

Information before court

Sources of information about being a witness

All VIWs were asked, unprompted, where they had received information about being a witness before they went to court. In phase 2, one in seven VIWs (14%) said they did not receive any information before going to court, 38 per cent mentioned the police, 23 per cent the Witness Service, 17 per cent a leaflet, and nine per cent Victim Support. Smaller proportions of VIWs mentioned the Court Service (7%) and the CPS or other lawyers (4%) as sources of information, while five per cent had got information from people they knew personally (family, friends and colleagues for example). Responses given by VIWs in phase

2 were similar to those given in phase 1, although a smaller proportion recalled being given information from a leaflet (17% compared with 26% in phase 1).

Phase 2 witnesses in the Crown Court were more likely than those in magistrates' courts to have been given information by the police (48% compared with 30%), while 20 per cent of witnesses in magistrates' courts mentioned a leaflet, compared with 13 per cent of Crown Court witnesses. Those who had received information before going to court were more likely to report overall satisfaction compared with those who did not receive such information (71% compared with 55%).

When prompted, only 26 per cent of child witnesses recalled receiving the Young Witness Pack (also referred to as Child Witness or Family Pack)[18] before going to court. In phase 1, 40 per cent of child witnesses recalled receiving such a pack.

Level of information

VIWs were asked if they had received enough information on the following issues before they went to court:

- how much time being a witness would involve;

- what to bring to court;

- what time they needed to arrive at court;

- directions to the court;

- what to do on arrival at court; and

- what would happen in court.

Figure 2.2 shows the proportion of VIWs considering that they had received enough information about various aspects of their court experience for the two survey years.

The level of information VIWs received varied greatly depending on its type. For example, although most were given enough information about what time they needed to arrive (94%

---

18 The pack contains a number of leaflets and booklets for young witnesses (aged from 5 to 17) designed to help them understand the court process and thereby help them give best evidence, together with a booklet for their parents/carers and (for the first time) a detailed handbook for practitioners. The pack is given out by the police.

in phase 2) and sufficient directions to the court (77%), fewer were given enough information about how much time attending court would involve (37%) and what to bring to court (42%). In Chapter 7, it is observed that giving evidence is one of witnesses' greatest concerns. However while 57 per cent of VIWs said they were given enough information about what would happen in court, 25 per cent said they were not given any information and 18 per cent felt they needed more information than they were given.

Although there is a very slight downward trend in the proportion of VIWs saying that no information was provided for some of the items given in the chart below, none of these differences are statistically significant.

Figure 2.2:   Level of information given before court

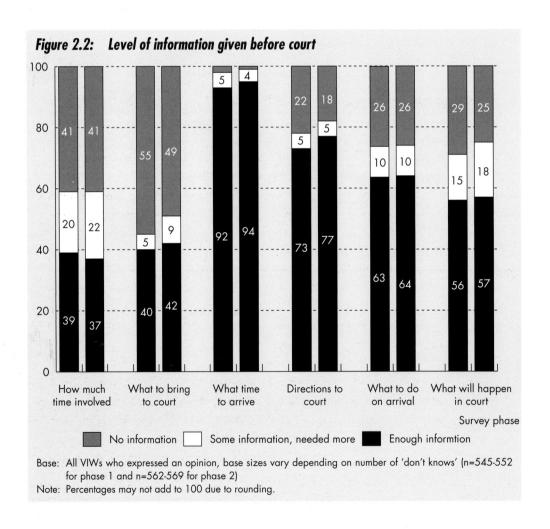

Base: All VIWs who expressed an opinion, base sizes vary depending on number of 'don't knows' (n=545-552 for phase 1 and n=562-569 for phase 2)

Note: Percentages may not add to 100 due to rounding.

Bringing a companion to court

Eight in ten VIWs in phase 2 were aware that they could bring a companion to court with them, either because they already knew (13%) or because they were told they could (67%). However, this left 20 per cent unaware that they were allowed to bring someone with them (no change from 2000). Unsurprisingly, most child witnesses in phase 2 were told that they could come with a companion (82%) or assumed this anyway (8%).

Support before court

All VIWs were asked about support which they had been offered or received before court. VIWs were asked about this in three different stages:

- did the police tell them about any organisations that could give them support?

- did they ask for any support or help from any organisation before they (or the child witness) went to court?

- were they offered any support by any organisations before they went to court?

In each question, a list of organisations including Victim Support, Witness Service, National Society for the Prevention of Cruelty to Children (NSPCC) and Rape Crisis was presented to the respondents, although they could also add the name of any other organisation.

The comparative figures for the two survey years are shown overleaf in Table 2.3.

In both survey years, around three-fifths recalled being given contact details of at least one organisation by the police, with around a fifth asking one of these organisations directly for support, and a third being offered support from them.

According to VIWs, the police were most likely to refer witnesses to Victim Support, in accordance with the formal policy to refer victims of certain offences to Victim Support[19]. They actually told 46 per cent about Victim Support in phase 2, though less than half of these actually had contact as a result (39%). The police were less likely to give contact details for the Witness Service, although there has been a significant rise in the proportion

---

19 Under the Victim's Charter (Home Office 1996) details of victims of burglary, assault, robbery, theft (except of and from cars), arson, harassment or damage to the victim's home are usually passed automatically by the police to Victim Support. In the case of sexual offences, domestic violence and homicide, details are only passed on if the victim agrees.

since 2000 (from 20% to 30%). The fact that the police are less likely to refer the Witness Service than Victim Support is unsurprising given that no formal system of referral exists between the police and Witness Service (the formal process is between the CPS and the Witness Service). However, it should be noted that Victim Support does liaise with the Witness Service if they are still supporting a victim when the trial takes place.

Table 2.3: Organisations providing support before court

Base: All VIWs excluding those saying don't know	Witness given contact details by police		Witness asked for support		Organisation offered support	
	Phase 1 (n=552) %	Phase 2 (n=547) %	Phase 1 (n=547) %	Phase 2 (n=565) %	Phase 1 (n=533) %	Phase 2 (n=552) %
Any	57	62	23	22	33	35
Victim Support	43	46	12	11	17	17
Witness Service	20	30	6	10	16	20
Rape Crisis	2	1	8	1	1	*
NSPCC	2	2	1	1	*	*
Other	5	5	6	5	3	3
No contact with police	3	4	n/a		n/a	

All VIWs who had either received or been offered help from any of these organisations were asked about the nature of help or support received. Table 2.4 shows the nature of support and help that VIWs received from Victim Support and the Witness Service before court in both survey years (base sizes for other organisations too low to report).

Information was the most common type of help provided by both Victim Support (56% in phase 2) and the Witness Service (69%) before court. This was followed by counselling: 20 per cent of those who had contact with Victim Support and ten per cent who had contact with the Witness Service said they had been provided with counselling. In fact "counselling" is probably something of a misnomer, as although both organisations provide emotional support and practical help and information, their staff are not trained counsellors.

Around three in ten of those in contact with Victim Support said that the organisation did not provide them with any help or support; this is not necessarily a "failure" of Victim Support – it could be that victims were referred to Victim Support but in the event they did not consider themselves to require any help from this organisation. Nine per cent of those in contact with the Witness Service said that they received no help. When comparing the phase 2 results with those in phase 1, VIWs were somewhat less likely to report receiving specific types of help, although only the fall in the proportion of VIWs receiving "counselling" from the Witness Service is significant.

Table 2.4:   Support received by Victim Support and Witness Service[20]

Base: All VIWs in contact with organisation excluding 'don't knows'	Victim Support		Witness Service	
	Phase 1 (n=163)	Phase 2 (n=166)	Phase 1 (n=124)	Phase 2 (n=152)
	%	%	%	%
Information	66	56	77	69
Counselling	29	20	19	10
Accompanied witness to court	16	10	27	37
Pre-trial visit	1	2	3	9
Somewhere to stay	2	1	3	7
Other	5	5	6	4
No help provided	19	28	10	9

In phase 2, of those who had received any help or support from Victim Support most (84%) found Victim Support helpful, (57% 'very helpful'). Similarly 93 per cent of those who had received any help or support from the Witness Service found it helpful (72% 'very helpful'). It is worth noting that there has been a slight fall in positive ratings for Victim Support amongst those using their services. In phase 1, 94 per cent rated the service as helpful, this falling ten percentage points to 84 per cent in phase 2.

However, user ratings are still high and this suggests that both organisations are providing the kind of support that vulnerable witnesses need before going to court, and there is a need to focus more on provision of referral information by the criminal justice agencies and defence lawyers to the Witness Service than on improving their services to existing contacts.

---

20 Note that these figures are based on all VIWs in contact with each of these organisations, rather than all VIWs in total. Thus, this explains why the figure for pre-trial visits is much lower than that reported later in this chapter, which is based on a more specific question asked of all VIWs.

Reasons for not asking for help or support

All VIWs who did not ask for and were not offered support by any organisation, but said that they would have liked it before going to court, were asked why they did not request any support. Responses were recorded in witnesses' own words, and later coded into categories. In phase 2, one in three (34%) said that they did not know support was available, 22 per cent said they did not know where to go to find the support they wanted, while a further 18 per cent said that they were unaware that they could ask for support as a witness. This suggests that a significant proportion of vulnerable witnesses need more information about what support is available and how to obtain it. The pattern of responses is very similar for the two survey years.

Pre-trial familiarisation visit to court

A significant minority of VIWs had actually visited the court before the trial to familiarise themselves (28% in phase 2, 29% in phase 1). This rose to 68 per cent per cent for victims of sexual offences (phase 2 data). VIWs in phase 2 who used any of the special measures for vulnerable and intimidated witnesses (as laid down in the 1999 Act) were also more likely than average to have been on a pre-trial visit (37%).

Of those VIWs who did not have a pre-trial visit, 63 per cent were not aware that these could be organised, and 59 per cent said that they thought such a visit would have been helpful (again phase 2 data).

In phase 2, VIWs who took up the opportunity of a pre-trial visit were asked how helpful they found this. The large majority (91%) found these visits helpful (73% 'very helpful'). When probed for why this visit had been helpful, most said simply that it had been helpful to know what they could expect in advance (81% of those finding visit helpful), while 24 per cent said that the visit helped ease their nerves and seven per cent mentioned becoming familiar with the television live link facility.

Support or help VIWs would have liked

All VIWs were asked, unprompted, if there was any kind of support or help they would have liked before court that they did not receive. In phase 2, 55 per cent of all VIWs said there was none. The most common responses for those who did have an opinion in the two survey years are shown in Table 2.5.

Table 2.5: Extra support VIW would have liked

Base: All who would have liked more support (excluding 'don't knows')	Phase 1 (n=228) %	Phase 2 (n=243) %
Information about what happens in court	21	23
More support (unspecified)	20	16
To be kept better informed	19	10
Someone to talk to	16	13
Counselling	8	5
Pre-trial court visit	8	5
Action to deal with intimidation/threats	7	5
Being accompanied to court	6	3

For those that would have liked more help in phase 2, information was a key requirement with 23 per cent saying they would have liked more information about what happens in court and ten per cent saying they would like to have been kept better informed. One in six wanted more support, presumably meaning more than they actually received.

Key points

- In both phases, over two-thirds of victims and witnesses said that they either experienced or feared intimidation, although experience of intimidation was self-defined and did not always relate to direct threats or actions by others; sometimes this was linked to a more general anxiety about what might happen. The main sources of intimidation experienced concerned the defendant and his/her family and friends. For example, in phase 2, 36 per cent of intimidated victims and witnesses were actually threatened by the defendant and 21 per cent by his/her family or friends.

- Intimidation most commonly occurred before cases reached court but also occurred while waiting at court. Compared with phase 1, victims and witnesses in phase 2 were less likely to feel intimidated while giving or waiting to give evidence.

- The police got to know about two-thirds of instances of intimidation. There was a slight rise in the proportion of victims and witnesses intimidated before court, who felt the police had dealt effectively with their intimidation (from 33% in phase 1 to 39% in phase 2) and there was a decrease in instances of intimidation where the police were considered to take no action (from 45% to 32%).

- Nine in ten VIWs in contact with the police considered that the police had treated them with courtesy, and eight in ten said that the police had given them sufficient support when they gave their statement. Satisfaction with the level of support given by the police was a strong indicator of overall satisfaction and willingness to act as a witness again.

- In phase 2, 36 per cent of VIWs were not kept informed about the progress of the case, compared with 27 per cent who were kept regularly informed. Being kept regularly informed was associated with overall satisfaction.

- The level of information received varied greatly depending on type of information. In phase 2, 94 per cent said they were given enough information about time of arrival at court but only 37 per cent were given enough information about the amount of time involved in attending court.

- The main sources of information about being a witness before going to court were: the police, Witness Service, a leaflet and Victim Support. In phase 2, 14 per cent received no information before going to court.

- In phase 2, 28 per cent of VIWs had a pre-trial court familiarisation visit; most (91%) found this helpful.

- In phase 2, over half of VIWs did not want any more information. Those who did want more information wanted: information on what happens in court (23%), more support generally (16%), someone to talk to (13%) and being kept better informed (10%).

This chapter examines what happened when VIWs attended court, including assistance in getting to court, contact with the Witness Service, facilities, and waiting times.

Changes to court dates

All VIWs were asked if the date they were originally given for the court case was subsequently changed. A large proportion of VIWs (45% in phase 2, 47% in phase 1) said that the date had been changed. In both surveys, VIWs at the Crown Court were more likely to say this than those at magistrates' courts (57% compared with 36% in phase 2).

In 35 per cent of cases in phase 2, dates were changed on the actual day the trial was due to take place, and on the day before in a further ten per cent of cases. In the remaining 55 per cent of cases where dates had changed, VIWs were given more notice.

All VIWs who said the original date was changed on the actual day or the day before were asked how this affected their feelings about going to court. In phase 2, sixteen per cent said it made them think about changing their mind about going to court, and 36 per cent said that the change in date made them feel more upset and anxious about going to court. Twenty-four per cent of VIWs had been annoyed by the change of date but it had not changed their feelings about going to court, and the same proportion indicated that it did not really bother them.

VIWs were also asked if they were given a reason for this change. Most (78%) said that they were, an improvement on the phase 1 survey when 69 per cent were given a reason. In phase 2, for the first time, VIWs whose court date had been changed were asked why. Seven per cent did not know the reason. The principal responses are shown in Figure 3.1.

VIWs who had not been given a reason for a change in date were slightly more likely to say they were dissatisfied with their overall experience than those who had been (40% dissatisfied compared with 30%)[21] and this pattern was consistent in both surveys

---

21 Difference not significant.

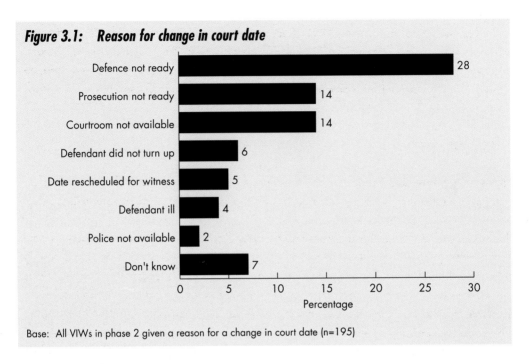

Figure 3.1: *Reason for change in court date*

Base: All VIWs in phase 2 given a reason for a change in court date (n=195)

Assistance getting to court

All VIWs in the survey were asked if an escort was offered or provided to go with them to or from court (for example from Victim Support or the police)[22]. In phase 2, nineteen per cent had been offered an escort, although a slightly lower proportion (16%) actually used one. Escorts were mainly used for the journey to court (15%) rather than from court (6%).

Use of escorts rose to 35 per cent among victims of sexual offences in phase 2. Escorts were provided to accompany 24 per cent of VIWs at the Crown Court, but only nine per cent at magistrates' courts.

Escorts provided were usually police family liaison officers (67%), or other volunteers (22%). Six per cent of this subgroup mentioned the Witness Service. Almost all VIWs using such an escort found them helpful (98%). About two in five VIWs (39%) who were not given an escort to or from court said they would have found it helpful.

Thirteen per cent of VIWs in phase 2 needed some kind of help in getting to court, for example, if they had mobility or transport problems. VIWs in social grade E were more likely

---

22 The equivalent figures on escorts in phase 1 have not been shown due to a slight change in wording for these questions which could have affected trends. Also, some questions in this section were asked for the first time in phase 2.

than other groups to report needing help getting to court (21%). Victims of sexual offences, and those with a physical disability or illness were also more likely to say that they needed help getting to court (21% and 27% respectively). About half of those who said they needed help were offered help from an official source (47%), mainly through transport being provided.

Dealing with VIWs' queries

All VIWs who attended court were asked, unprompted, who was available in court to deal with any queries they had (Figure 3.2). Some mentioned more than one type of person.

The majority of VIWs in phase 2 said that the Witness Service had been available to deal with queries (60%). A further six per cent mentioned Victim Support. Some of these may have meant the Witness Service, as they may have been aware of the Witness Service as representatives of Victim Support. In addition 18 per cent said that the police were available in court to assist with their queries. Nine per cent mentioned court staff in general, 11 per cent specifically mentioned ushers, ten per cent mentioned the court receptionist, and ten per cent referred to a lawyer or the CPS. Nine per cent of VIWs said that they had no queries, while only two per cent said that no one was available to deal with their queries. The pattern of responses was similar in both surveys.

Figure 3.2: **Who dealt with queries at court**

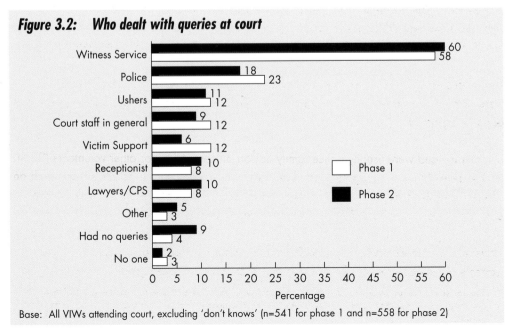

Base: All VIWs attending court, excluding 'don't knows' (n=541 for phase 1 and n=558 for phase 2)

The Witness Service

In the survey, a brief description of the Witness Service (WS) was given, and VIWs were asked about any contact they had had with the Witness Service and what support it had provided. Those who did not have contact with the Witness Service were asked if they would have liked any support as a witness. The results on all these questions were very similar in both surveys; thus this section discusses the results from phase 2.

A fifth of VIWs (22%) said they had contact with the Witness Service both before and after arriving at court. Unsurprisingly given its remit, just six per cent of VIWs recalled having contact with the Witness Service only before going to court, while 61 per cent said they had contact while they were at court, but not before. Eleven per cent of VIWs claimed that they had no contact at all with the Witness Service. Approaching half (49%) of those VIWs who did not have any contact with the Witness Service said they would have liked some support as a witness while they were at court.

All VIWs who recalled contact with the Witness Service were asked whether they had asked for support or been offered it. Most VIWs (89%) said that the Witness Service had offered them support, with just 11 per cent saying they themselves had requested support.

The overwhelming majority of VIWs who had experienced contact with the Witness Service felt they had given them support ("support" was described as practical help, giving explanations, and providing reassurance or calming them down). Eighty per cent of VIWs in this group said they had 'definitely' been given such support, while 17 per cent said they had been given support 'to some extent'.

VIWs who had contact with the WS after arriving at court were asked when support was provided by the Witness Service. Nearly all (96%) said that this was whilst they were waiting to give their evidence. Some had received support at more than one stage: 35 per cent of VIWs who gave evidence said that the Witness Service had given them support while they were in the courtroom giving evidence and 58 per cent that they had been supported after giving evidence. The lower proportion given support in the courtroom probably reflects the fact that the time-consuming task of supporting someone while they give evidence has to be balanced against the possibility of providing other support to a greater number of people out of the courtroom.

All VIWs who had contact with the Witness Service were asked if the WS had been able to explain everything they did not understand about being a witness. The majority (88%) said that the Witness Service had been able to do this, with only five per cent saying this was not the case. Seven per cent said they had understood everything, so did not need any explanation.

Facilities in court

All VIWs in phase 2 were asked if they were satisfied in general with the facilities[23] at court. The majority (81%) said that they had been generally satisfied with the facilities. In phase 1, certain subgroups only – specifically those with a physical disability and those affected by intimidation – were asked this question so trend comparisons can only be made on the basis of these subgroups. Among those with a disability, satisfaction with facilities has increased only slightly from 68 per cent to 74[24] per cent , although for those fearing or experiencing intimidation, satisfaction has increased more noticeably from 66 per cent to 77 per cent.

VIWs who were satisfied with the facilities were more likely to be satisfied with their experience overall than those who were not (73% compared with 48%).

In phase 2, as in phase 1, concerns about intimidation appeared to be the most common reason for dissatisfaction with the court facilities. Of those VIWs who were dissatisfied with facilities in phase 2, 21 per cent said that this was because the defendant or defence witnesses were using the same facilities, while 18 per cent complained that in order to reach the facilities they had to pass through the area where the defendant was waiting.

For those fearing or experiencing intimidation there has been an encouraging reduction in the proportion dissatisfied for the above reasons. Based on all affected by intimidation and dissatisfied, 37 per cent complained about defendant/defence witnesses using the same facilities in phase 1, this reducing to only 20 per cent in phase 2.

More general complaints about the facilities included: lack of refreshments (mentioned by 11%); quality of food (8%); and the state of the toilets (8%).

Being accompanied at court

Most VIWs[25] (83% in phase 2, 81% in phase 1) said that someone had accompanied them to court. Unsurprisingly, among witnesses in phase 2 aged under 17 this figure was

23 Including toilets, refreshments and waiting areas.
24 Not significant.
25 Excluding proxy interviews and those where parents/relatives answered for child witnesses.

higher, at 99 per cent. Three fifths (61%) of witnesses were accompanied by a parent, and this rose to 92 per cent among those aged under 17. A quarter (24 %) brought another relative with them, 21 per cent a friend, and 16 per cent were accompanied by their spouse or partner.

VIWs who were accompanied at court but responded to the survey interview on their own behalf were asked whether they were able to have the person accompanying them with them whenever they wished. Respondents taking part in the interview on a witness's behalf were asked if they or whoever accompanied the witness were able to be with them whenever they wanted.

In both instances, most said they were able to have the accompanying person with them whenever they wanted (73% and 81%). Seventeen per cent of accompanied VIWs said this was not possible because the person accompanying them was also a witness, and this was also the response given by six per cent of parents/guardians answering on behalf of a witness. Ten per cent of accompanied VIWs and 13 per cent of parents/guardians said they could not always have the person accompanying with them, even though this person was not a witness.

Waiting to give evidence

All VIWs were asked if, when they attended court, they were told approximately when their case was likely to be heard. Most VIWs in phase 2 (75%) said they were told this each time they attended. Five per cent said they were only told on some occasions, while 20 per cent said they had never been told what time the case would be heard. VIWs who were always told when the case would be heard were more satisfied than those who were given no information (71% compared with 58%). The pattern of responses was similar in both surveys.

VIWs who actually gave evidence were also asked how long they had to wait in court before being called. There was considerable variation. In phase 2, a fifth (23%) waited an hour or less, a third (32%) between one and two hours, while 22 per cent waited between two and four hours, and 23 per cent waited longer than four hours. VIWs at magistrates' courts tended to have shorter waiting times, with 28 per cent only waiting up to an hour, and just 15 per cent waiting more than four hours. A similar pattern was found in the phase 1 survey, and can probably be attributed to the greater length and complexity of cases in the Crown Court, together with lengthier cross-examination, which make it more difficult to predict when a particular witness will be called to give their evidence. Victims tended to wait for less time than other prosecution witnesses (27% waited up to an hour compared with 16% of other prosecution witnesses in phase 2), probably because victims are likely to be called earlier than other witnesses.

VIWs' views of how long it is reasonable to wait were similar in both surveys, with three-fifths (61%) in phase 2 expecting to wait no longer than an hour and only five per cent thinking a wait of more than two hours was reasonable. VIWs with higher expectations tended to be more dissatisfied. There was no evidence of a relationship between having a disability or illness and perceptions of how long it is reasonable to wait. Most VIWs (69%) said they were kept informed of progress at least once an hour while they were waiting, although 12 per cent had been given no information.

Seeing the defendant outside the courtroom

A large proportion of victims and other prosecution witnesses (46% in phase 1, 44% in phase 2) said that they had not been able to avoid seeing the defendant when they were not in the courtroom. This figure was particularly high, at 53 per cent, for prosecution witnesses who said they had experienced intimidation in phase 2. There was no difference between witnesses in the Crown Court and those who attended magistrates' courts.

Table 3.1 looks at where VIWs had seen the defendant outside the courtroom: in both surveys the most common place was waiting outside the courtroom (74% in phase 1, 67% in phase 2 which equates to 29% and 34% respectively of all prosecution witnesses). This is in spite of the fact that 95 per cent of VIWs (94% in phase 1) reported that there were separate waiting rooms for prosecution and defence witnesses. This suggests that just providing a separate waiting room does not prevent the problem, when other facilities may still have to be shared. Chapter 6 discusses further the separation of defence and prosecution witnesses for intimidated witnesses.

Table 3.1: Where prosecution witnesses saw defendant

Base: All prosecution witnesses who saw defendant	Phase 1 (n=247) %	Phase 2 (n=247) %
Saw waiting outside courtroom	74	67
Saw in toilets	24	14
Saw in canteen	20	19
Saw on the way to/home from court	n/a	25
Saw elsewhere	35	17

Courtroom familiarisation

A large proportion of VIWs in phase 2 were given the opportunity to look around a courtroom either on the day of trial (53%) or before the hearing (28%). Eight per cent were given the opportunity of having a familiarisation visit but did not take this up. This leaves 32 per cent (28% in phase 1) who were not given the opportunity to see a courtroom before they gave evidence, even if they might have wanted to.

Days attended court without giving evidence

A total of 59 per cent of VIWs (60% in phase 1) were called to court on more days than they were actually required to give evidence. Overall, 39 per cent were called to court but did not give evidence at all, while 20 per cent did give evidence but were called to court on more days than were required. The reasons why such a large proportion were called to court but were not in the event required to give evidence are detailed at the beginning of Chapter 4 (this shows that the principal reason was a change by the defendant to a guilty plea).

Of those VIWs who did give evidence, forty-one per cent in phase 1 were called to court on more days than they were actually required to give evidence. However, this figure had reduced to 33 per cent in phase 2. Of the subgroup of VIWs in phase 2 who gave evidence but were called to court more times than needed, 20 per cent were called on one extra day, seven per cent on two, and six per cent attended on three or more further days than were required.

Reading statements before giving evidence

Reading their statement through or having someone read it to them while waiting to give evidence may help witnesses refresh their memories of events which often happened months before the case came to court. The vast majority of VIWs who made a written statement either saw their statement (90%) or had someone read it to them at court (3%) – no change from phase 1.

As detailed in Chapter 2, in the phase 2 survey one in five VIWs (20%, mainly children) said they had made a video-taped statement. Of these, 44 per cent were given the chance to watch the video in court, and 23 per cent at an earlier stage. Thirty-five per cent were, however, not able to see the video at all. Chapter 6 contains further details about video-recorded evidence-in-chief.

Contact with lawyer

In phase 2, six per cent of prosecution witnesses who gave evidence (no change from phase 1) said they did not know who the prosecuting lawyer was. Of those who did, a sizeable minority (32%) said they had no contact with the prosecuting lawyer other than being questioned in the courtroom, although this had fallen from 43 per cent in phase 1. Among those who had contact in phase 2, the majority (59%) said it was on the day of the case with only eight per cent reporting contact before the day. In both phase 1 and phase 2, VIWs in magistrates' courts were much more likely than VIWs in the Crown Court to recall having contact with the prosecuting lawyer (76% compared with 59% in phase 2).

In phase 2, three out of four prosecution witnesses (76%) who had no contact before the trial would have liked to meet the prosecuting lawyer before going into the courtroom.

Of those who had contact, a quarter (26%) did not have any questions they wanted to ask the lawyer, 58 per cent had had their questions answered and 16 per cent said the lawyer did not answer their questions.

Alterations to the charges

All VIWs were asked whether the original charges against the defendant were changed at any point and, if so, how. While it is important to collect VIWs' perceptions of such changes as this may influence satisfaction, it should be noted that such information provided by VIWs may not be wholly reliable. Table 3.2 shows the proportion of VIWs who said that the original charges against the defendant were changed during the case and in what ways.

Table 3.2:   Whether original charges changed

Base: All VIWs	Phase 1 (n=552) %	Phase 2 (n=569) %
Yes – charges upgraded	4	4
Yes – charges downgraded	13	15
Yes – additional charges	2	2
Yes – charges cut	5	8
Yes – changed but not sure how	4	5
No, no changes	58	57
Don't know	15	12

Table 3.2 shows that there were no significant differences between phase 1 and phase 2. Most VIWs in phase 2 (57%) said that no changes were made to the original charges against the defendant, while a few (12%) were not sure if the charges had changed or not. When charges were changed, it was most commonly to downgrade or reduce them in number, or to cut them with 23 per cent saying this had happened. Just six per cent said that the charges had been upgraded or extra charges added. Five per cent of VIWs said that charges had been changed but they were not sure in what way.

As in phase 1, a quarter (24%) of VIWs in phase 2 who did not give evidence said that the original charges were downgraded, compared with just eight per cent of those who gave evidence, indicating this may have been the reason for some VIWs not being needed to give evidence (i.e., defendant pleaded guilty to lesser charges). In phase 2 as in phase 1, downgrading of charges appeared to be associated with overall satisfaction, with 40 per cent of those saying this had happened being dissatisfied, compared with 26 per cent of VIWs who thought there to have been no changes to the original charges.

Key points

- Nearly half of VIWs stated that the original date set for the court hearing had been changed. In phase 2, in almost half of cases this occurred on the day of the trial (35%) or the day before (10%)

- In phase 2, late changes to the date led to feelings of upset and anxiety (36%), annoyance (24%) and thoughts about changing their mind about going to court (16%). A further 24 per cent were not bothered by the change.

- In phase 2, 19 per cent of VIWs had been offered an escort to/from court and 16 per cent had used an escort.

- Only 11 per cent of VIWs did not have any contact with the Witness Service – about half of these VIWs would have liked some support at court.

- Concerns about intimidation appeared to be the most common reason for dissatisfaction with court facilities. In phase 2, 21 per cent dissatisfied VIWs said this was because the defendant or defence witnesses used the same facilities and 18 per cent said that in order to reach facilities they had to pass through the area whether the defendant was waiting.

- There was a wide variation in waiting time to give evidence. In phase 2, 23 per cent of VIWs waited up to an hour, 32 per cent between one and two hours, 22 per cent between two and four hours and 23 per cent waited longer than four hours.

- Seeing the defendant was often unavoidable – around half of victims and other prosecution witnesses had seen the defendant outside the courtroom and a similar proportion of intimidated victims and witnesses has seen the defendant outside the courtroom.

- In phase 2, 53 per cent of VIWs were given the opportunity to look around the court on the day of the trial.

- The vast majority of VIWs who made a written statement were given their statement to read before giving evidence or had someone else read it to them.

- The proportion of victims and prosecuting witnesses who had no contact with the prosecuting lawyer, other than when they were questioned in court, decreased from 43 per cent to 32 per cent between phase 1 and 2. Many victims and prosecuting witnesses would have liked to have met the prosecuting lawyer beforehand.

- Downgrading of charges was associated with overall satisfaction, with 40 per cent of VIWs in cases where charges had been downgraded being dissatisfied compared with 26 per cent of witnesses who thought there to have been no changes to the original charges (phase 2).

This chapter examines the experience of giving evidence and cross-examination, including questioning by lawyers and contact with the judge or magistrate. Many VIWs interviewed (61%) said they actually gave evidence; this is slightly lower than the proportion who had given evidence in phase 1 (68%). As in phase 1, VIWs at the Crown Court were more likely to report having given evidence than those at magistrates' courts (65% compared to 57%). Also a higher than average proportion of victims of sexual offences reported giving evidence (83%).

In phase 1, VIWs who had given evidence tended to be more satisfied than those who had not (67% satisfied compared with 56%). However, in phase 2 VIWs who had not given evidence were marginally more likely to be satisfied than those who had (73% satisfied compared to 67%)[26]. Unlike in phase 1, there was evidence of a relationship between whether they gave evidence and whether they would be willing to act as a witness again. As might be expected, VIWs who had given evidence tended to be less happy about being a witness again compared to those who had not given evidence (39% happy compared to 52%).

Reasons for not giving evidence

Table 4.1:   Reason given for not being required to give evidence

Base: All VIWs who did not give evidence at all	Phase 1 (n=177) %	Phase 2 (n=224) %
Defendant pleaded guilty	75	78
Prosecution dropped case before trial	4	7
Case collapsed after hearing started	5	5
Defendant did not turn up	1	1
Defendant charged with a lesser crime	-	1
Other	7	4
No reason given	5	4

As Table 4.1 shows, in around three-quarters of cases where VIWs did not have to give evidence, they thought this was because the defendant pleaded guilty. In a smaller proportion of cases, VIWs did not need to give evidence because the prosecution dropped the case

---

26 Difference not significant.

before the trial was underway (7% in phase 2) or the case collapsed after the hearing started (5%). Just one per cent of VIWs who did not give evidence said that this was because the defendant did not turn up, and a further one per cent said that the defendant was charged with a lesser crime. Four per cent of those who were not required to give evidence were not given any reason for this. These proportions are in line with the results of the phase 1 survey.

The remainder of this chapter details findings based on all those who gave evidence. As there were so few defence witnesses in the samples who gave evidence (n=9 in phase 1, n=4 in phase 2) the following analyses based on the experiences of VIWs with their lawyers and during cross-examination only include the experiences of victims and prosecution witnesses.

Questioning by prosecution lawyer

Victims and other prosecution witnesses were asked if they felt they had the opportunity to say everything they wanted to when being questioned by the lawyer for 'their side' (i.e., the prosecution). Most (75% in phase 1, 77% in phase 2[27]) felt they did have the opportunity to say everything they wanted to, in response to questioning by the lawyer for the same side. However, 19 per cent in phase 2 felt that they had not had this opportunity, of which 39 per cent said that this was because they did not get a chance to explain in more detail and give all the facts.

In phase 2, only 47 per cent of phase 2 prosecution witnesses who did not feel they were able to say everything they wanted were satisfied with their overall experience, compared with 71 per cent of those who felt they were given enough opportunity. This mirrors the result in phase 1.

As in phase 1, the vast majority (95%) of phase 2 prosecution witnesses felt that the prosecution lawyer was courteous towards them, and there was no significant difference between victims and other prosecution witnesses.

Cross-examination by defence lawyer

In both phases, almost all victims and prosecution witnesses who gave evidence (94%) said that they were asked questions by the lawyer acting for the 'other side' (i.e., the defence). In phase 2, one witness said they were not, as the defendant represented him/herself, while

---

27 These figures are based on all who gave evidence including 'don't knows'. Five per cent said 'don' know' in phase 1 and three per cent in phase 2.

six per cent said the defence did not question them at all. (Cross-examination by the defendant is discussed further in Chapter 6.)

Thirteen per cent of phase 2 prosecution witnesses who were cross-examined did not know in advance that this would happen (an increase from nine per cent in phase 1)[27]. This might have been because lawyers assumed that their witnesses would already know about cross-examination.

Two-thirds (66%) of phase 2 victims and other prosecution witnesses who were cross-examined felt that the defence lawyer had not been courteous towards them when questioning them about their evidence. This increased from just over half (55%) of victims and other prosecution witnesses in phase 1 who felt that this was so.

Treatment by the defence lawyer appears to be associated with general satisfaction, with 83 per cent of phase 2 victims and other prosecution witnesses who were treated courteously saying that they were satisfied, compared with 55 per cent of those who did not think they were treated courteously. Similarly, 51 per cent of those who said the defence lawyer had been courteous said they would be willing to be a witness again, compared to just 32 per cent of those who thought they were not treated courteously. This pattern of response was very similar to that in phase 1.

In phase 2, 43 per cent of victims and prosecution witnesses cross-examined felt they had been given the opportunity to say everything they wanted in response to questioning by the defence lawyer, a decline from 53 per cent of such witnesses in phase 1. Male witnesses were more likely than females to feel this (52% compared with 38%). In phase 1, fewer victims felt the defence lawyer had given them the opportunity to say everything they wanted compared to other prosecution witnesses (43% compared to 67%). Although the same was true in phase 2, it was to a lesser extent (41% compared to 47%)[28].

Of the 57 per cent who felt they were not given the opportunity to say everything, 43 per cent said that this was because the lawyer interrupted or cut off the witness. Similarly, a further 23 per cent said that they did not get a chance to explain and give all the facts.

On the whole, the findings show that victims and other prosecution witnesses in phase 2 were less happy with their treatment by the defence lawyer than the equivalent group of witnesses in phase 1. These findings can be related to the finding quoted in Chapter 7 which shows a significant fall in the satisfaction ratings concerning the defence lawyer between the two surveys.

28 Difference not significant.

Respite during cross-examination

Most prosecution witnesses in phase 2 (86%) did not have any problem standing while they gave evidence, but 14 per cent said that they did have difficulty. Six in ten (60%) of the 49 VIWs who had some kind of physical disability said that they had difficulty standing. Of the 49 VIWs who had difficulty standing to give evidence, 36 told someone about this difficulty, and 41 were allowed to sit in the witness box while they gave evidence. This mirrored the results from phase 1.

Table 4.2: Whether VIW had a break or felt able to ask for a break

Base: All victims and prosecution witnesses who gave evidence	Phase 1 (n=344) %	Phase 2 (n=341) %
Yes, had break	23	31
No, but felt able to ask	37	40
No, and didn't feel able to ask	35	28
Don't know	5	1

For witnesses with physical problems, a mental illness or learning disabilities, or suffering from the stress of giving evidence, having a break during cross-examination may be important. The results are similar in both phases, although VIWs in phase 2 were slightly more likely to have been given some respite (31% compared with 23% in phase 1). VIWs in phase 2 were also slightly less likely to say that they did not have a break and did not consider that they were able to ask for one (28% compared to 35% in phase 1).

As in phase 1, more VIWs at the Crown Court recalled that they actually had a break than in magistrates' courts (46% compared to 18%); this might be attributable to a longer period of questioning in Crown Courts, because of the more serious nature of the offences they deal with. Also mirroring the phase 1 survey, victims were more likely than other prosecution witnesses to have had a break (39% compared to 18%), and victims of sexual offences were also more likely to have had a break (61%). It is likely that these victims would be more likely to be in need of a break due to the more sensitive nature of the questioning.

Impact of cross-examination

As shown in Table 4.3, most victims and prosecution witnesses (71%) who were cross-examined said that the experience had upset them (no change from phase 1, 69%).

As in phase 1, those subgroups particularly likely to be upset by their experience of cross-examination were women (58% experiencing "a lot" of upset compared with 31% men), victims (53% compared with 38% of other prosecution witnesses) and in particular victims of sex offences (66%). However, child witnesses were less likely than those in other age groups to say they were upset with cross-examination, with only a third (35%) in phase 2 saying the experience had upset them "a lot".

Table 4.3:   Whether being questioned upset the witness in any way

Base: All prosecution witnesses questioned by defence lawyer/defendant	Phase 1 (n=344) %	Phase 2 (n=306) %
Yes, a lot	46	48
Yes, a little	23	23
No	31	29

It is relevant to note that those who used special measures were slightly less likely to have been upset "a lot" compared to all prosecution witnesses (38% and 48% respectively), although this was not statistically significant.

VIWs' feelings about being cross-examined are related to their opinion about the whole experience. While less than half (45%) of those in phase 2 saying the cross-examination had upset them "a lot" were satisfied overall; this rose to 76 per cent and 91 per cent respectively among those who said that cross-examination had only upset them "a little" or "not at all".

Figure 4.1 shows the reasons given for being upset by the process of cross-examination. Only reasons mentioned by more than three per cent of VIWs are shown.

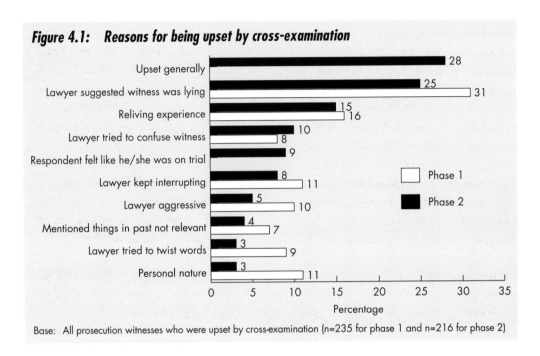

Figure 4.1: *Reasons for being upset by cross-examination*

Base: All prosecution witnesses who were upset by cross-examination (n=235 for phase 1 and n=216 for phase 2)

Other than general upset caused by the experience, the aspect of cross-examination that VIWs most commonly said upset them was the lawyer suggesting they were lying, with a quarter (25%) in phase 2 mentioning this, which was down from 31 per cent in phase 1. This was especially true of child witnesses (32 per cent). Fifteen per cent of prosecution witnesses said they had been upset because being questioned made them relive the experience of the offence, while nine per cent said that it felt like they were on trial themselves.

Most of the other reasons cited for being upset by cross-examination also related to the behaviour of the lawyer. Ten per cent of prosecution witnesses said the lawyer tried to confuse them or 'trip them up', eight per cent said the lawyer kept interrupting them, while five per cent said the lawyer's manner was aggressive. Three per cent said that the lawyer twisted their answers. Smaller proportions said they had been upset because the lawyer brought up issues from their past (4%), while three per cent said that the personal nature of the case had made being cross-examined upsetting.

Contact with judge or magistrate

All VIWs who gave evidence (including the small number of defence witnesses) were asked about their contact with the judge or magistrate. Six in ten VIWs who gave evidence (60%

in phase 2) said that the judge or magistrate spoke to them while they were giving evidence. As might be expected, more VIWs in the Crown Court than in the magistrates' court said that the judge or magistrate had spoken to them (78% compared to 44%). Also, victims were more likely than other prosecution witnesses to have been spoken to by the judge or magistrate (63% compared to 55%). As in phase 1, nearly all VIWs (98%) who were spoken to by the judge or magistrate while they were giving evidence felt the judge or magistrate had treated them with courtesy.

A new question was added to the phase 2 survey asking whether VIWs felt that they had been given an opportunity to say everything they wanted to say when being questioned by the judge or magistrate. The vast majority (90%) felt that this was the case, five per cent felt they had not been given the opportunity and the remaining five per cent did not express an opinion.

Ninety-eight per cent of those who had video-taped evidence played in court, and 96 per cent of those who had used a live television link said that they had been given the opportunity to say everything they wanted to say by the judge or magistrate.

Understanding of questions and accuracy of evidence

Some vulnerable witnesses (e.g., child witnesses, those for whom English is not their first language, and those with learning or communication difficulties) may have problems in their comprehension of the questions asked during cross-examination.

Table 4.4: *Whether questions were asked in a clear and straightforward way*

Base: All VIWs who gave evidence excluding 'don't knows'	Phase 1 (n=357) %	Phase 2 (n=340) %
Yes, always	52	46
Some were, some weren't	36	47
No	12	7

Table 4.4. shows that of those VIWs who gave evidence in phase 2, 46 per cent felt that the questions they were asked had always been clear and straightforward, while a further 47 per cent said that some questions were clear and straightforward, but that others were not. Compared with phase 1, phase 2 VIWs were slightly less likely to say that all questions were clear but a similar proportion said that at least some of them were clear. Just under

half (44%) of child witnesses said the questions asked of them were always clear and straightforward, while a similar proportion (46%) said that some were but others were not. Four in ten (39%) of those who had been a victim of a sexual offence felt that the questions asked were always clear and straightforward. There were no significant differences between witnesses who had and had not given evidence using a special measure.

As was the case in phase 1, VIWs who did not feel all questions asked were clear were more likely to be dissatisfied with the experience than those VIWs who had full comprehension of the questions (46% compared to 18%).

Most VIWs who gave evidence (87% in both phases) felt they could have asked for questions to be explained. Only 13 per cent in phase 2 said they did not feel able to do this. As Figure 4.2 shows, around nine in ten VIWs who gave evidence in both surveys felt that they understood everything that went on, either 'very' or 'quite' well, while around one in ten felt they did not understand everything. VIWs who felt that they understood everything either 'very' or 'quite' well were less likely to be dissatisfied with their experience as a witness compared to those who understood less (29% compared to 68%). This mirrored the phase 1 survey findings. Similarly those with the greater understanding were more likely to say that they would be happy to be a witness again (42% compared to 18% of those with more limited understanding).

Figure 4.2: *How well VIWs understood everything*

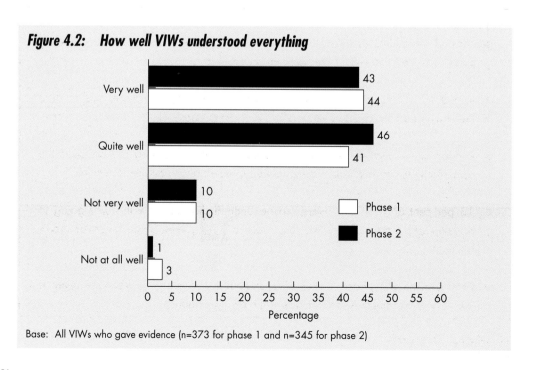

Base: All VIWs who gave evidence (n=373 for phase 1 and n=345 for phase 2)

Less than half of VIWs (46% both phases) felt they had given their evidence completely accurately, in the sense that they had been able to recall adequately and convey to the court their recollections of what they had seen. In phase 2, a further third (33%) felt it had been fairly accurate and just over a fifth (21%) of VIWs who gave evidence did not feel they had been able to give their evidence at all accurately. Women were slightly more likely than men to feel that their evidence had not been accurate (23% compared to 17%)[29]. Child witnesses were slightly more likely than other witnesses to feel they had been able to give their evidence accurately, with 53 per cent saying it was completely accurate[30]. VIWs who had used a special measure to give evidence were more likely to say that they had been able to give their evidence completely accurately compared to VIWs not using measures (52% compared to 39%).

Not surprisingly, feeling able to give evidence accurately appears to be related to satisfaction with the overall experience of being a witness. Eighty-three per cent of those saying they had been able to give their evidence completely accurately were satisfied with the experience compared to 31 per cent of those who did not feel this. Similarly, 51 per cent of those who considered that their evidence had been given completely accurately were happy to be a witness again, compared with only 25 per cent who did not feel this.

Key points

- Around three-fifths of VIWs surveyed gave evidence. The defendant pleading guilty was the main reason for not giving evidence.

- In phase 2, VIWs who did not give evidence were marginally more satisfied than those who had testified (the reverse of the trend in phase 1).

- Around one in five VIWs giving evidence considered that they did not have the opportunity to say everything they wanted to when giving evidence-in-chief.

- 13 per cent of VIWs who were cross-examined did not know this was going to happen and nearly three-quarters were upset by their experience of cross-examination.

- Over one-third in phase 1 and over one-quarter in phase 2 were not given a break and felt unable to ask for one while giving evidence.

---

29 Difference not significant.
30 Difference not significant.

- Two-thirds of phase 2 victims and prosecution witnesses thought the defence lawyer had not treated them with courtesy and over half had not given them adequate opportunity to say everything they wanted.

- Treatment by the defence lawyer is associated with general satisfaction. In phase 2, 83 per cent of victims and prosecution witnesses who considered that they were treated courteously were satisfied overall, compared with 55 per cent for those not considering this.

- Almost nine out of ten VIWs had at least a reasonable understanding of what was going on in court.

- A little less than half of VIWs who gave evidence felt they had given their evidence completely accurately – those who had were more satisfied with their overall experience and more willing to be a witness again, compared to VIWs who had not felt they had given their evidence accurately.

- There appeared to be an association between special measures and cross-examination. Compared with VIWs not using them, VIWs who used special measures were less likely to be upset by cross-examination, and more likely to say they had been able to give their evidence completely accurately.

5   Experiences after giving evidence

This chapter examines the experiences of VIWs once they have finished giving evidence, covering issues such as support while still at court and later their views on the verdict and practical details such as claiming of expenses.

Before leaving court

Three in ten VIWs in phase 2 (30%) said they were not told what would happen after they had finished giving evidence (no change from phase 1, 33%). Women were more likely than men to say that they had been given such information (73% compared with 65%)[31]. As was the case in phase 1, being given such information was associated with satisfaction. Seven in ten (71%) of those who were told what would happen when they finished giving evidence were satisfied with the experience, compared to 56 per cent of those who were not told.

As in phase 1, most VIWs (73%) said that someone (other than a friend or relative) spoke to them before they left court. Once again, female VIWs were more likely than male VIWs to say this (79% compared with 64%). Eighty-four per cent of victims of sexual offences said someone spoke to them to check they were all right, but fewer of those who experienced intimidation said this (69%). It seems likely that this is because victims of sexual offences are more easily identified than witnesses who have been intimidated. VIWs who gave evidence were more likely to have been spoken to by someone before they left court than those who did not (77% compared with 67%), perhaps because it was assumed that giving evidence is potentially more upsetting than attending and not giving evidence.

VIWs who were spoken to before they left court were more likely to have been satisfied with the experience compared with those who had no such interaction (71% compared with 62%).

VIWs who had spoken to someone before leaving court were asked who this was. As in phase 1, this was most commonly a representative of the Witness Service, with 77 per cent saying this was the case. About a quarter (23%) said that a police officer spoke to them, while eleven per cent said that they were spoken to by a member of the court staff. Smaller proportions mentioned lawyers (9%), Victim Support (5%) and NSPCC (1%).

---

31 Difference not significant.

Twenty-seven per cent of VIWs in phase 2 had not interacted with any official before leaving court. These VIWs were asked whether they felt they did in fact need help of any kind. A quarter (25%) of this group expressed unmet needs with regard to help on leaving court, a slight reduction on the equivalent proportion (35%) in phase 1.

Verdict

Figure 5.1 shows the verdicts that VIWs said were reached in the cases in which they appeared.

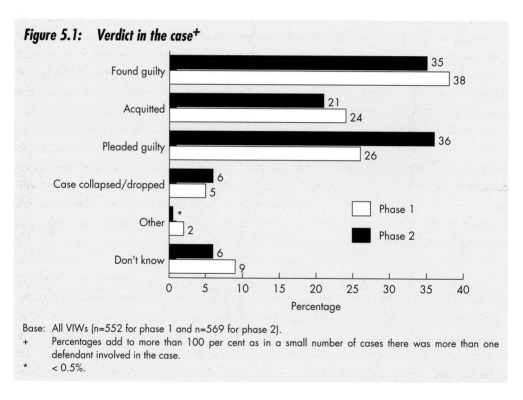

Figure 5.1: Verdict in the case[+]

Base: All VIWs (n=552 for phase 1 and n=569 for phase 2).
+ Percentages add to more than 100 per cent as in a small number of cases there was more than one defendant involved in the case.
* < 0.5%.

In phase 2 compared with phase 1, there has been a drop in the overall proportion of contested cases (from 62% to 56%), with a corresponding increase in the proportion of cases where the defendant pleaded guilty (from 26% to 36%). This is linked to the finding that a somewhat smaller proportion of VIWs gave evidence in phase 2 (61%) compared with phase 1 (68%). In 21 per cent of cases the defendant was acquitted (no significant change from phase 1). Just two per cent of VIWs said that the case was dropped before the hearing started, and three per cent said the case collapsed after the hearing had started.

In phase 2, victims of sexual offences were more likely than other witnesses to say the defendant had been acquitted (39 per cent). Also, defendants were far more likely to plead guilty at magistrates' courts (42%) compared with Crown Courts (26%).

Unsurprisingly, the verdict in the case is related to satisfaction, with 74 per cent of VIWs in cases where the defendant was found guilty or pleaded guilty being satisfied compared to 57 per cent of VIWs where the defendant was acquitted. This mirrors the findings of the phase 1 survey.

A slight majority of VIWs in phase 2 (55%) thought that the verdict of the case was fair compared with 43 per cent who considered it unfair. In phase 1, opinion on the fairness of the verdict was split more equally, with 47 per cent of VIWs saying they thought the verdict was fair compared with 49 per cent thinking it unfair. Part of the reason for the small increase in the proportion regarding the verdict favourably may be explained by an interview instruction added in phase 2 which asked the interviewer to clarify that the question was about the verdict and not the sentence.

As in phase 1, more VIWs in magistrates' courts thought the verdict was fair, compared to those in the Crown Courts (62% compared to 45%). This is possibly related to the higher conviction rate in magistrates' courts. Only 35 per cent of victims of sexual offences thought the verdict was fair: this may be related to the high acquittal rate for sexual offences. Given that most VIWs in the sample were prosecution witnesses, these differences are in line with the proportion of acquittals given.

Perhaps unsurprisingly, only five per cent of phase 2 VIWs in cases where the defendant was acquitted thought the verdict was fair, whereas when the defendant was found guilty, 78 per cent thought this was fair. As might be expected, those who considered the verdict to be fair were more satisfied than those who considered the verdict to be unfair (79% compared to 57%). However, the fact that 21 per cent of those who considered the verdict to be fair were still dissatisfied indicates that aspects of the experience of being a witness, other than the final outcome, influence satisfaction.

Two-thirds (66%) of VIWs said they were told the verdict compared to just over half (55%) of VIWs in phase 1, while the remainder found out for themselves. In phase 2, VIWs aware of the verdict most commonly said they found out the verdict from the police (29%), followed by the CPS or lawyer (15%) and Court Service (13%). The Witness Service and Victim Support also occasionally told VIWs (8% and 3% respectively). One in ten VIWs found out by watching the case (9%), but slightly more (13%) were told by a relative, friend or neighbour and three per cent found out from another witness. A small proportion (2%) of VIWs heard about the verdict through the media. These findings are very similar to those in phase 1.

VIWs in the Crown Court were more likely than those in magistrates' courts to have found out the verdict from the police (44% compared with 18%). In contrast, those in magistrates' courts were more likely to hear from the CPS or other lawyers (20% compared with 9%), and also more likely to hear from the Court Service (19% compared to 6%). Again, this mirrored the results from the phase 1 survey. Just over a quarter of VIWs in phase 2 (27%) who did not give evidence were told the verdict in the case by the CPS or another lawyer, while only seven per cent of those who gave evidence found out this way.

Follow-up support

All VIWs who attended court were asked if they were provided with details of follow-up support and, if not, whether they would have liked such support (Table 5.1).

Table 5.1:   Whether given details of follow-up support

Base: All who attended court (excluding 'don't knows')	Phase 1 (n=541) %	Phase 2 (n=558) %
Given details	29	34
No, but would have liked follow-up support	29	26
No, but did not want follow-up support	42	41

There was a small (non-significant) difference in the proportion of VIWs saying that details about follow-up support were given (from 29% to 34%). These details were most commonly provided by the Witness Service (63% of those given details of support), the police (19%) and Victim Support (17%). Twenty-six per cent of VIWs said that they would have liked follow-up support after being at court, but were not given any details (29% in phase 1). A similar proportion (30%) said they were not given details and did not need any follow-up support, while ten per cent said that they did not want any information about follow-up support.

Expenses

VIWs in phase 1 were asked about their experience of claiming expenses, although these questions were not repeated in phase 2.

In phase 1, 40 per cent of VIWs claimed expenses, of whom 66 per cent said that this covered their costs (6% did not know whether their costs had been covered). Thus only just over a quarter of VIWs claimed expenses which covered all the costs they incurred as a witness. A further 11 per cent claimed expenses but said this did not cover all their costs. About half (53 per cent) of VIWs had not claimed expenses but knew that they could have done, while only seven per cent had not claimed and were not aware that they could claim expenses for being a witness. These figures show a high level of awareness that expenses could be claimed. More VIWs in Crown Courts (53%) claimed expenses, compared to those in magistrates' courts (19%). One possible reason for this difference might be that, because cases take longer to complete in Crown Courts, witnesses incur greater expenses and are therefore more inclined to claim them. Where expenses were considered to have fully met costs, the witness was more likely to be satisfied (68%) than where this was not the case (47%).

Key points
- Three in ten VIWs said they were not told what would happen after they had finished giving evidence. Witnesses who were told what would happen tended to be more satisfied.

- Three-quarters of VIWs in phase 2 said that someone – most commonly the Witness Service – spoke to them before they left court to check that they were all right. This experience was positively associated with satisfaction.

- The proportion of VIWs who were told the verdict increased from 55 per cent in phase 1 to 66 per cent in phase 2. The nature of verdict was strongly associated with satisfaction, with 74 per cent of VIWs in cases where the defendant was found guilty being satisfied compared with 57 per cent of VIWs where the defendant was found not guilty at phase 2.

- In line with expectations, VIWs who considered that a fair verdict had been reached were much more likely to be satisfied overall than those who did not consider this. However, 21 per cent of those who considered the verdict to be fair were still dissatisfied, indicating that aspects of the experience of being a witness, other than the final verdict, influenced satisfaction.

- A third of VIWs were given details of follow-up support while at court, a small increase from phase 1. A further 26 per cent of VIWs said that they would have liked follow-up support after being at court, but were not given any details.

- In phase 1, 40 per cent of VIWs claimed expenses. VIWs were more likely to be satisfied when the expenses fully met costs compared to when costs were not fully met.

6   **Measures to assist witnesses**

This chapter looks at the extent to which measures to help vulnerable and intimidated witnesses (VIWs) give best evidence are now being used, whether those who did not receive such measures would have found them useful, and attitudes to the special measures that have already been introduced under previous Acts (e.g., the Criminal Justice Acts of 1988 and 1991) and those that are in the process of being introduced under the Youth Justice and Criminal Evidence Act 1999. It also examines intimidation and the extent to which VIWs are consulted about the provision of measures to assist them.

Throughout this chapter, measures are clearly indicated as being either "special measures", that is those which are part of the 1999 Act legislation, or simply "other forms of assistance" which means that there is no statutory footing. Background to this legislation is detailed in Chapter 1.

Measures before the court hearing

Interpreters and intermediaries
An *interpreter* may be used to facilitate communication between the witness and the police or the court, when English is not the first language of the witness or the witness does not have a sufficient command of English to communicate with the court. Interpreters are responsible for providing an accurate transfer of meaning from one language to another. They must not explain the questions to the witness nor explain the witness's answers. They are, however, allowed by their code of conduct to intervene to ask for clarification, accommodation of the interpreting process and to alert all the parties to possible misunderstandings and missed cultural inferences. They will then interpret any subsequent explanations.

An *intermediary* is a person who facilitates communication between the police, prosecution and defence legal teams and/or the court and a vulnerable witness to ensure that the communication process is as complete, coherent and accurate as possible. They may be used to help a witness who has difficulty understanding questions or answering questions clearly and coherently to communicate. As stated in the Youth Justice and Criminal Evidence Act 1999, they may "explain such questions or answers so far as necessary to enable them to be understood by the witness or person in question". As yet, intermediaries are not available for vulnerable witnesses. However, preparations are underway for the provision of intermediaries to be piloted before national implementation. The pilot began in March 2004 and is expected to run for 18 months in six police force sites (starting with Merseyside Police).

VIWs with some form of communication difficulty[32] were asked whether they needed an interpreter, signer or other person (intermediary) who could help them communicate their statement to the police. The need for such a service was very low with just one and two per cent respectively of VIWs with some form of communication difficulty in phase 1 and phase 2 in need of an interpreter when giving their statement. A further one and two per cent respectively said that they needed an intermediary. No VIWs said that they needed a signer.

In phase 2, children were also asked about any need for any of the above measures; only four children (2%) said that this was a requirement.

Video-recorded evidence-in-chief

The Criminal Justice Acts of 1988 and 1991 allowed child witnesses to give evidence-in-chief by means of video recordings made prior to the trial unless the court considered that, in the interests of justice, a recording or any part of it ought not to be admitted in any particular case. Video recordings can benefit young children with limited language skills as well as providing a fuller picture of how the child responded to questioning.

The use of video-recorded evidence among all child witnesses[33] rose from 30 per cent in phase 1 to 42 per cent in phase 2[34]. Under the Youth Justice and Criminal Evidence Act 1999 the special measure of video-recorded evidence-in-chief will be available to a wider group of children and to adult vulnerable and intimidated witnesses as well as children. However, full implementation of the provision is still awaited and at the time of the phase 2 survey this measure had been introduced in Crown Courts for section 16 (vulnerable) witnesses only and in magistrates courts' for child witnesses in need of special protection only (defined by section 21 of the 1999 Act). Therefore in phase 2, adults were also asked whether they had been given the opportunity to give video-recorded evidence-in-chief. Only 15 adults in phase 2 (5%) said that this was the case.

---

32 This included those with a disability affecting their communication, witnesses for whom English was not their first language, as well as witnesses with a mental health problem or learning difficulty.
33 Including those who did not go on to give evidence.
34 In phase 2, a fuller explanation of this measure was given. Witnesses were told: "The police sometimes video-tape interviews with witnesses in advance, so that they do not have to stand up in court and give evidence, although they may still be cross-examined about it".

Among the 111 (mainly child) witnesses in phase 2 who had given video-recorded evidence-in-chief, support for this special measure was very high with 91 per cent finding it helpful. VIWs finding this special measure helpful were asked why. The main reasons were:

- Not having to appear in court (43%).

- Easier to say things (22%).

- Less scared (13%).

- Helped witness to remember (12%).

- Friendly/comfortable environment (9%).

All adult and child witnesses in the phase 2 survey who did not have the opportunity to give evidence in this medium (n=437) were asked whether they would have found this helpful. Almost half (48%) of these witnesses said that they would have found this helpful if available. This represents 38 per cent of all witnesses.

Three-quarters (72%) of phase 2 VIWs who had given a pre-recorded video statement also gave evidence. Of these 80 VIWs, 84 per cent (n=67) said that the video was played in court, while ten per cent said that it was not and six per cent were not sure.

Video recorded pre-trial cross-examination

One special measure under the Youth Justice and Criminal Evidence Act 1999 that had not been implemented at the time of the phase 2 survey was the use at trial of pre-recorded cross-examination of vulnerable witnesses. In the phase 1 survey, most (72%) of the VIWs thought it would be helpful to have the cross-examination process recorded on video before the trial instead of being questioned during the trial. Fifty-three per cent said this would be 'very helpful'. Victims were more likely than other prosecution witnesses to think this special measure would be useful (77% compared with 67%).

Assistance at court

Escort to and from court

Escorts (other form of assistance) are sometimes provided by the police, and less frequently by other agencies such as the Witness Service. Escorts may be particularly helpful for intimidated witnesses and those with mobility problems, but many other witnesses might also find having an escort reassuring. In both surveys, one in five VIWs (20% in phase 1, 19% in phase 2) said they had been offered an escort either to or from the court. Around one in seven (13% phase 1, 16% phase 2) actually used an escort.

In both surveys, provision of escorts was more common in the Crown Court than in magistrates' courts (24% compared with 9% in phase 2). Use of escorts rose to 35 per cent among victims of sexual offences, although witnesses who had experienced intimidation were no more likely than other groups to have been offered an escort.

In phase 2, VIWs were asked about who had been their escort. Escorts provided were usually police family liaison officers (67%), or other volunteers (22%). Six per cent of this subgroup mentioned the Witness Service. Almost all VIWs using such an escort found them helpful (98%). As in phase 1, about two in five VIWs (39%) who were not given an escort to or from court said they would have found it helpful. Witnesses who experienced intimidation were more likely than other groups to say that they would have found an escort helpful (50% of this subgroup). VIWs who did not have an escort but would have appreciated one were more likely to be dissatisfied overall (45%) compared with those who had no such unmet need in this respect (24%).

Pagers

Pagers (other form of assistance) are sometimes used so that witnesses do not have to wait in court (which can possibly involve sharing a waiting room and/or other facilities with the defendant and his or her supporters) but instead can wait nearby until they are called to give evidence. Mobile phones can perform the same function. However, no VIWs in either survey reported being provided with a pager or mobile phone, although two per cent in both cases reported using their own mobile phone.

In phase 1, 50 per cent of all VIWs who attended court said that a pager or mobile would have been helpful. However, the level of interest in this form of assistance rose to 64 per cent in phase 2, possibly as a result of greater familiarisation with mobile phone and pager technology. However, it is also likely to be related to a change in question wording. In phase 2, VIWs were given an explanation as to why pagers and mobile phones might be useful[35]; it is possible that in phase 1 (no such explanation), not all witnesses appreciated their potential use.

Communication in the courtroom

Child witnesses and witnesses with communication problems may sometimes find it helpful to be offered communication aids such as communication boards, computers or dolls. In phase 1, all witnesses who gave evidence and were aged under 17 or said they had a learning disability, a physical disability affecting communication, psychological or emotional problems, or difficulty speaking English were asked if this special measure was used to assist them in the courtroom. Only six per cent of these witnesses had actually used some form of communication aid in the courtroom. In phase 2, the base changed and all VIWs who gave evidence were asked this question. However, the level of usage was still very low with only four per cent (n=11) of VIWs giving evidence using communication aids.

Use of interpreters and intermediaries at court

The need for interpreters, signers or other intermediaries was negligible in both surveys. In phase 2, only three per cent of witnesses with communication difficulties (n=6) needed an interpreter at court, while a further one per cent (n=2) needed another kind of intermediary. One witness needed a signer in court. Five child witnesses (2%) needed assistance of this kind. These results are similar to those for use of interpreters at the point of giving a statement, as discussed in Chapter 2.

Of these thirteen witnesses, nine said that an interpreter or intermediary was organised for them at court, while three organised their own, and one said that none was organised. Nine of the twelve witnesses who had an interpreter/intermediary said that they met this person before going into the courtroom. All twelve found having an interpreter or intermediary helpful.

Giving evidence via a live television link

Under the Criminal Justice Act 1988 [initially for those aged under 14; extended to those under 17 years in sex offence cases under the 1991 Act] certain child witnesses in the Crown Court and youth court could be questioned from the courtroom via a live TV link with

---

35 The following explanation was given: "Pagers and mobile phones mean that witnesses can leave the court building and go somewhere else (e.g. to the shops) but still be contacted".

a special separate room, as an alternative to giving evidence in the courtroom[36]. This meant that although the defendant and counsel could see and hear the witness, witnesses did not have to see the defendant but only the lawyer questioning him/her. This was thought to be less intimidating for the witness than giving live evidence in the courtroom. The 1999 Act further extended the facility to a wider group of children and to adult vulnerable and intimidated witnesses (although it remains to be fully implemented).

In the phase 1 survey, of those child witnesses who gave evidence, 43 per cent were given the option of using a live TV link. For those not given this opportunity, this may have been because it was decided to hear the case in an adult magistrates' court, where there was normally no provision for this facility prior to the 1999 Act, rather than the youth court or Crown Court. Another possible reason could be changes to charges, so that the case no longer came within the scope of those for which the live TV link was available at the time.

However, the picture was very different in phase 2, with the availability of live TV link doubling to cover 83 per cent of child witnesses. In phase 2, adult witnesses giving evidence were also asked about whether this option had been offered and a further 29 witnesses (15% of adult witnesses giving evidence) said this was the case. In total, 46 per cent of all VIWs who gave evidence in phase 2 were offered this facility.

As in phase 1, the majority (87%) of those offered the option of using the live TV link in phase 2 actually used it, and all but three (2%) of those who did use it said that the live TV link was explained to them before they gave evidence. All but three of the 135 VIWs who used the live TV link in phase 2 said that someone was in the live link room with them while they gave evidence: this was mainly someone from the Witness Service (50%), an usher (34%) or a parent (16%).

Most (87%) of those who used the live link said that the room made them feel comfortable, and 90 per cent said that they found it helpful to give their evidence in this way. The main reason given for why such a measure was useful was because they appreciated the ability to give evidence without having to see the defendant or anyone else in court.

All VIWs who had not been offered the option of using the live TV link were asked how helpful they would have found it to give evidence in this way. Most (57%, unchanged from phase 1) said that they would have found it 'very' or 'quite' helpful to give evidence via a live TV link. Rather more female than male VIWs said they would have found a live TV link

---

36 This provision only applied to witnesses aged under 17, for sexual offences or ones involving violence or cruelty. For those aged under 14 it also covered neglect.

very helpful (67% compared with 41%). Witnesses experiencing intimidation who had not had the option of using this special measure were also more likely to feel that this would have been helpful (68%).

Screens

The courts also had discretion prior to the 1999 Act to have screens placed around the witness box to prevent the witness from being able to see the defendant, while still allowing him/her to see the judge or justices, legal representatives and any interpreter (and vice versa). Again anecdotal evidence suggests this discretion was rarely used. The 1999 Act places this power on a statutory footing.

All VIWs who gave evidence without a live TV link were asked if screens were used: the proportion of this subgroup using this special measure rose from only three per cent in phase 1 to 13 per cent in phase 2. This means that the proportion of VIWs giving evidence who did not have to see the defendant either through using a live TV link or through the use of screens rose nearly three-fold between phase 1 and phase 2, from 17 per cent to 47 per cent.

Of the 27 VIWs in phase 2 using screens, 20 were witnesses at Crown Court, nine were aged under 17, and 22 had either feared or experienced intimidation. Screens were generally appreciated, with 22 out of the 27 VIWs using this special measure finding it helpful.

VIWs who did not have the opportunity to use either live TV links or screens were asked whether they would have found screens helpful. There was a fairly high level of support for this special measure with 60 per cent saying it would have been helpful, especially women (70% compared with 46% men), and those experiencing intimidation (71%).

Figure 6.1 summarises the change in use of screens and live TV links between the two surveys, as well as the proportion of those not using either of these special measures who would have found screens useful. Figures are based on all VIWs giving evidence. The increase in the use of these special measures has reduced the level of unmet need with regard to screens from 50 per cent to 31 per cent of VIWs giving evidence. The need for facilities such as screens was clearly very high with only a fifth (21%) in phase 2 saying that they would not have found this special measure helpful.

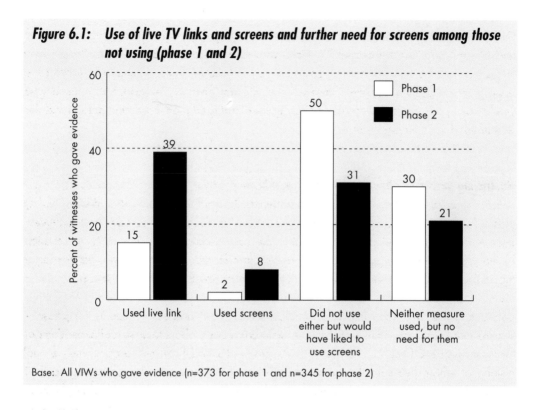

Figure 6.1: **Use of live TV links and screens and further need for screens among those not using (phase 1 and 2)**

Base: All VIWs who gave evidence (n=373 for phase 1 and n=345 for phase 2)

Clearing the public gallery

Even before the 1999 Act, the courts in England and Wales had discretion – although anecdotal evidence suggests it was rarely used – to order that some or all of the evidence be heard without the public and press being present. The 1999 Act places this power on a statutory footing for cases involving sexual offences or those involving intimidation. A nominee of the press would be able to stay although it would be open to the court to impose reporting restrictions under section 46 of the 1999 Act (not yet implemented).

In phase 1, all victims of sexual offences and witnesses who said they were intimidated were asked whether the public gallery was cleared while they gave evidence. Ten per cent said it had been – nine per cent of those who were intimidated and seven per cent of sex offence victims. In phase 2, these proportions were virtually unchanged (11% and 7%). Although in phase 2 this question was also asked of other vulnerable and intimidated witnesses, these were the only types of witness to use this special measure. As many as 18 per cent did not know or could not remember whether the gallery was cleared.

Of the small group of 32 witnesses for whom the gallery had been cleared in phase 2, most (n=30) said they found it helpful. Of those who said it had not been cleared, 29 per cent thought it would have been helpful, while 24 per cent did not know whether this would have been helpful for them. Of the witnesses who did not have a cleared gallery, those who would have preferred this were more likely to be dissatisfied than those who did not feel this was needed (49% compared to 28%).

Restricting questions about sexual or medical history

In the past there have been concerns that evidence of complainants' sexual or medical history (in the latter case including details of contraception or abortions) was sometimes admitted, even where this was not directly relevant to the case. Section 41 of the 1999 Act restricts lawyers from questioning complainants of sexual offences about their previous sexual or medical history, unless various criteria are met which establish relevance to the case.

Before the changes came into effect, all adult victims of sexual offences in the phase 1 sample were asked whether they were questioned in court about their sexual experience or medical history. Of the 28 witnesses in this group, 13 had been asked about their sexual history, of whom five said they were asked about both their sexual experience and their medical history. The remaining fifteen did not recall being asked about either. In phase 2, after the changes came into effect, the picture is very similar (18 out of 38 witnesses said they were not asked about either). However, base sizes are so small that no meaningful conclusion can be drawn.

As in phase 1, views were evenly split on whether this was necessary or not (of the 20 in phase 2 asked about sexual or medical history, nine said yes, ten said no).

Removal of wigs and gowns

The courts also had discretion prior to the 1999 Act to order judges and lawyers to remove their wigs and gowns, where it is felt that this would help vulnerable witnesses give evidence. This special measure was mostly associated with child witnesses. The 1999 Act places this power on a statutory footing, where a court considers it will help a vulnerable witness give best evidence.

All Crown Court witnesses who gave evidence were asked whether wigs and gowns were removed. This was rare in both surveys, although the occurrence doubled from eight per cent in phase 1 to 15 per cent in phase 2. Wigs and gowns were removed more often for child witnesses (25% at phase 2).

In phase 2, most VIWs for whom wigs and gowns were removed (15 out of 24) said this was helpful. A further 14 per cent of those VIWs giving evidence at Crown Court for whom wigs and gowns were not removed said they thought this would have been helpful, while seven per cent were not sure.

Preventing defendants cross-examining witnesses

The 1999 Act prohibited defendants in cases involving sexual offences from cross-examining complainants in person. It also prohibited defendants from cross-examining child complainants and other child witnesses in cases involving sexual offences, violence, abduction and cruelty. There had previously been similar provision for children only. The relevant 1999 Act provisions, covering adults as well as children, came into effect in September 2000[37]. Another 1999 Act provision, implemented in July 2002, gives courts the power to impose a prohibition on a defendant from cross-examining any particular witness. This might be exercised, for example, in cases involving intimidation.

This happened very rarely in practice, with only six per cent of prosecution witnesses and victims giving evidence in phase 1 saying that they had been questioned by the defendant and seven per cent in phase 2. Nine of the 23 witnesses saying this had happened in phase 1 were aged under 17; similarly ten of the 24 witnesses who said this has happened in phase 2 were aged under 17. Four of the 23 in phase 1 were victims of sex offences. Most (n=14) thought it would be helpful to prohibit this practice in future.

It seems likely, however, that these figures are overestimates and that witnesses may have misunderstood the question in some way. The reason for suggesting this is that 17 of the 23 witnesses in phase 1 also said they were asked questions about their evidence by the defence lawyer. One possible explanation is that some VIWs were questioned by the defence lawyer initially, but the defendant later sacked the defence lawyer and represented him/herself subsequently. However, the discrepancy between the figures does throw some doubt on the reliability of these findings. In addition, in phase 2, seven of the 24 witnesses were involved in sex offence cases, and six children were involved in violence cases, which as explained above should not be possible. This provides further evidence that the results for this question may be not be wholly reliable. This is important because, if taken at face value, the findings suggest that some children were subjected to cross-examination by the defendant, when in fact this should not have happened.

---

37 The Home Office has commissioned a research project to examine the use of previous sexual history evidence in rape cases in order to determine how s.41 of the 1999 Act is working in practice. The project is due to be completed in summer 2004.

Measures to prevent intimidation at court

In Chapter 2 it was reported that 69 per cent of VIWs in phase 1 and 70 per cent in phase 2 either feared or experienced intimidation. In phase 2, 17 per cent feared intimidation and 53 per cent actually experienced it.

Witnesses in these categories were asked which out of a prompted list of measures had been put in place at court for them. In both surveys, a majority of these witnesses had had some form of assistance to help prevent intimidation – 72 per cent in phase 1 and 77 per cent in phase 2[38].

By far the most common measure was a separate waiting room for witnesses, with 68 per cent mentioning this in phase 1, 64 per cent in phase 2. When all VIWs were asked about separate waiting rooms, most (94% in phase 1, 95% in phase 2) said that separate rooms had been provided. Of the 28 VIWs in phase 2 saying both sides waited in the same area, seven said that attempts were made to keep the two sides separate, while 21 said no such attempt was made.

Only one in five (19% phase 1, 22% phase 2) said that they were given an escort to and from the court to prevent intimidation, while one per cent in both surveys said that they had an escort within the court. Other special measures used in court to prevent witnesses being intimidated were: screens in the courtroom (3% phase 1, 9% phase 2); and TV link (26% in phase 2 – this was not included as an option in phase 1).

Of those who had measures put in place at court to deal with intimidation, the majority felt that these measures had helped them in some way. In phase 2 (no change from phase 1), a quarter 25%) said that this completely stopped them feeling intimidated and 53 per cent said that it stopped them to some extent from feeling intimidated. Just 22 per cent said that the measures did not do anything to prevent their feelings of intimidation. Court measures seemed to be less successful in preventing intimidation among those who experienced it than those who feared it, with 25 per cent of those who experienced intimidation saying that court measures did not prevent them feeling intimidated at all, compared to 13 per cent of those who feared intimidation. Unsurprisingly, those saying that that court measures did not prevent them feeling intimidated were more likely to be dissatisfied (52%) than those who said that feelings of intimidation were prevented to some extent (35%) or completely (20%).

---

38 Difference not significant.

Table 6.1: How effectively intimidation dealt with at court

Base: All who felt intimidated at court	Phase 1 (239) %	Phase 2 (192) %
Very effectively	15	16
Quite effectively	33	38
Subtotal – effectively	47	54
Not very effectively	16	18
Not at all effectively	29	22
Subtotal – not effectively	45	41
Don't know	8	5

Table 6.1 shows that, in both phases, around half of witnesses who felt intimidated at court thought that the problem had been dealt with effectively[39]. Use of special measures appeared to be effective in dealing with this problem. Witnesses using special measures in phase 2 were more likely than those not using any measures to consider that the intimidation had been dealt with effectively (66% compared with 48%).

Witnesses who considered that their feelings of intimidation had been effectively dealt with were more likely to be satisfied (71% in phase 2) than those who did not (39% in phase 2).

What should have been done at court to prevent intimidation

Witnesses who felt intimidated at court and said that this had not been dealt with effectively were asked what they thought should have been done to prevent them feeling intimidated. The main issue with intimidation at court appears to be the problem of witnesses coming into contact with the defendant and their supporters. In phase 2, a quarter (25%) of those who felt that intimidation at court was not dealt with effectively said that they should not have had to see the defendant. About as many (27%) said that there should have been separate entrances and facilities, so that contact with those responsible for intimidation could have been avoided, and 29 per cent said that there should have been separate waiting rooms for prosecution and defence witnesses. Screens in the courtroom were mentioned by seven per cent, while eight per cent said that they did not think they should have been made to give evidence in the courtroom. Three per cent said that surveillance in court would have helped to prevent intimidation occurring. These findings remain unchanged from phase 1.

---

39 The rise from 47per cent in Phase 1 to 54 per cent in phase 2 is not significant.

The Home Office has funded a project to look at reluctant witnesses (e.g. due to intimidation). This project is being carried out at a local level by West Mercia Constabulary. The project is due to be completed in June 2004.

Consultation about special measures

The 1999 Act creates a requirement on the court to consider the views of vulnerable witnesses in decisions about special measures, and this is further emphasised in draft guidance aimed at all criminal justice agencies (Home Office, 2000). Figure 6.2 shows that there has been a significant rise in consultation. Thus, while only 12 per cent of witnesses in the phase 1 survey said that they were consulted about the use of measures, this rose nearly three-fold to 32 per cent in phase 2. In phase 2, as in phase 1, child witnesses were more likely to have been consulted (46%), as were those who attended Crown Court (38% compared with 28% in magistrates' courts). Consultation about the provision of measures was particularly high for victims of sexual offences (51%). Those fearing intimidation were more likely to have been consulted than those actually experiencing intimidation (42% compared with 28%).

Figure 6.2:   Whether witness consulted about use of special measures (phase 1 and 2)

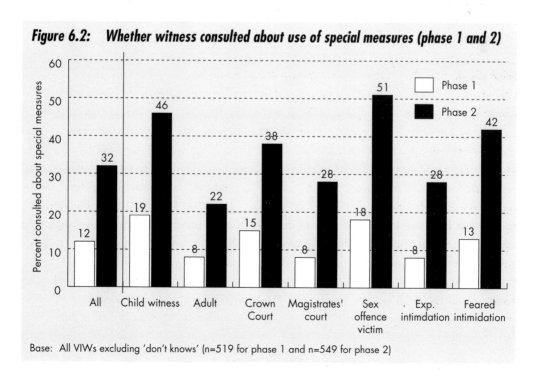

Base: All VIWs excluding 'don't knows' (n=519 for phase 1 and n=549 for phase 2)

Just over half (53%) of those consulted about measures actually used at least one of them (i.e., special measures such as screens, live TV link, and clearing the public gallery and other forms of assistance such as escorts and interpreters). Only a quarter (25%) of those not consulted used any of these measures.

VIWs in phase 2 who were consulted about the use of measures were asked about the extent to which they considered that their views had been taken into account. In total, nearly nine in ten (87%) said that their views had been acted on – 60 per cent said that "all of their views" had been acted upon and 27 per cent said that "some of their views" has been acted upon, leaving only 14 per cent who said that their views had not been taken into account.

Whether witness would have given evidence if special measures not available

In phase 2, VIWs who used at least one of the special measures (that is, video-recorded evidence-in-chief, live link, screens, clearing the public gallery, removal of wigs and gowns and communication devices) were asked:

"Thinking of the measures we have been talking about, do you think if these measures had NOT been available, you would still have been willing and able to attend court and give evidence?"

A third (33%) of those using special measures said that they would not have been willing and able to give evidence if these forms of assistance had not been available to them. Sixty one per cent said that the use of special measures did not affect their willingness and ability to give evidence, while the remaining six per cent were not able to give an opinion.

Sex offence victims using special measures were particularly likely to say that the measures enabled them to give evidence that they would not otherwise have been willing or able to give (44%).

Summary of use of special and other measures in phases 1 and 2

Table 6.2 gives a summary of the use of special measures in both pre- and post-implementation surveys. It also shows the proportion of all VIWs for whom the special measures were relevant and who would have liked to use them but were not given access to them. The table shows that use of most of the special measures has risen between phase 1 and phase 2, and in particular live TV link, video-recorded evidence-in-chief and removal of wigs and gowns. It also shows that the highest level of unmet need in phase 2 was for live TV link (34%) and screens (31%) – although witnesses would not require both of these special measures.

Table 6.3 shows the use of, and level of unmet need for other forms of assistance. There has been very little change in the level of usage of other forms of assistance. Among those not using these measures, pagers were the most popular type of assistance required.

Table 6.2: *Use of special measures and those not using these who would have liked to (phase 1 and 2)*

Type of measure	Phase 1		Phase 2		Base ('don't knows' are excluded)
	Used measure	Did not use but would have liked to	Used measure	Did not use but would have liked to	
	%	%	%	%	
Live TV link	15+	48	39	34	All VIWs who gave evidence (phase 1: n=373; phase 2: n=345)
Screens	2	50	8	31	All VIWs who gave evidence (phase 1: n=373; phase 2: n=345)
Video-recorded evidence-in-chief	30	28	42	28	All child witnesses (phase 1: n=177; phase 2: n=231)
Clearing public gallery	8	24	10	26	All VIWs who gave evidence (phase 1: n=373; phase 2: n=345)
Removal of wigs and gowns	8	20	15	12	All giving evidence at Crown Court (phase 1: n=208; phase 2: n=157)
Use of communication aids	4~	n/a	4	n/a	All VIWs who gave evidence (phase 1: n=373; phase 2: n=341)
Intermediaries	2	1	4	*	Witnesses with communication difficulties (phase 1: n=296; phase 2: n=209)

n/a Question not asked.
+ In phase 1, only child witnesses were asked about live TV link; however, this has been rebased on all giving evidence to ensure comparability with phase 2.
~ In phase 1, only children and witnesses with communication difficulties were asked about communication aids; however, this has been rebased on all giving evidence to ensure comparability with phase 2.

Table 6.3   **Use of other forms of assistance and those not using these who would have liked to (phase 1 and 2)**

Type of measure	Phase 1		Phase 2		Base ('don't knows' are excluded)
	Used measure	Did not use but would have liked to	Used measure	Did not use but would have liked to	
	%	%	%	%	
Use of pagers	-	50	-	64	All VIWs who attended court (phase 1: n=547; phase 2: n=567)
Separate waiting areas	94	n/a	95	n/a	All VIWs who attended court (phase 1: n=548; phase 2: n=566)
Pre-court familiarisation visits	29	n/a	28	25	All VIWs who attended court (phase 1: n=551; phase 2: n=567)
Escorts to/from court	13	30	16	32	All VIWs who attended court (phase 1: n=551; phase 1: n=569)

n/a   question not asked

Key points

- The use of interpreters, signers and other intermediaries was negligible.

- The use of video-recorded statements among witnesses aged under 17 rose from 30 per cent in phase 1 to 42 per cent in phase 2. In phase 2, nine in ten using this found it helpful.

- In phase 1, almost three-quarters of VIWs thought that it would have been helpful to have been cross-examined on videotape before the trial.

- A fifth (19%) of VIWs in phase 2 said they were offered an escort either to or from the court.

- The proportion of VIWs who thought that access to a pager or mobile phone in court would have been helpful increased from 50 per cent in phase 1 to 64 per cent in phase 2.

- In phase 1, 43 per cent of witnesses under 17 who gave evidence said they were offered use of a live TV link, this doubling to 83 per cent in phase 2. A further 15 per cent of adult witnesses in phase 2 were offered this facility. At phase 2, 90 per cent of all witnesses using this facility found it helpful.

- In phase 2, one in eight (13%) reported use of screens in court, up from only 3 per cent in phase 1. Sixty per cent of VIWs in phase 2 who did not have access to this facility or a live TV link thought they would have been helpful.

- Removal of wigs and gowns at Crown Court was relatively rare, although it increased from 8 per cent to 15 per cent between survey phases.

- Most of the VIWs for whom the public gallery had been cleared, thought this special measure was helpful.

- Around three-quarters of intimidated victims and witnesses had access to measures to help prevent intimidation at court. Half of these witnesses at phase 2 said that the intimidation they feared or experienced had been dealt with effectively.

- In phase 1, only 12 per cent of VIWs said they had been consulted about the use of measures currently available, although this rose nearly three-fold to 32 per cent in phase 2. Half (51%) of sex offence victims said they were consulted. At phase 2, 87 per cent of witnesses who were consulted about the use of measures said that their views had been acted upon at least to some extent.

- A third of VIWs in phase 2 who used special measures said that these enabled them to give evidence they would not otherwise have been willing or able to give. This figure was particularly high for sex offence victims (44%).

- Overall, the use of special measures had increased, in particular for live television link, video-recorded evidence-in-chief, and removal of wigs and gowns.

- The highest level of unmet need was for measures that resulted in the witness avoiding seeing the defendant such as screens and live TV link. However, the level of unmet need among VIWs giving evidence has reduced significantly from 50 per cent to 31 per cent between the survey phases.

7   Views about the experience of being a witness

This chapter examines VIWs' views and attitudes towards their experience as a witness. It looks at anxiety and distress caused by the experience, incidence of discrimination, satisfaction levels with different aspects of their experience, willingness to be a witness again, and confidence in the CJS.

Anxiety and distress

All VIWs were asked if at any point the experience of being a witness or the court environment had made them feel "really anxious or distressed". Figure 7.1 show overall levels of anxiety as well as what contributed to this: experiences before court, the court environment, or the experience as a whole (respondents could answer 'yes' to any of these).

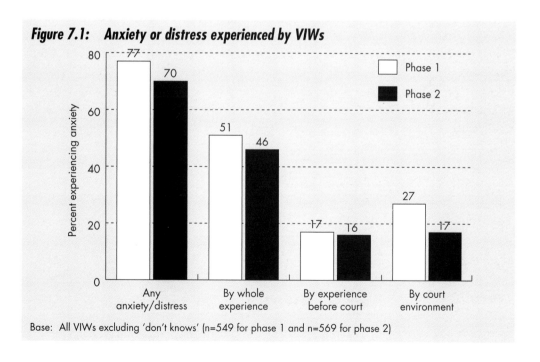

Figure 7.1:   Anxiety or distress experienced by VIWs

Base: All VIWs excluding 'don't knows' (n=549 for phase 1 and n=569 for phase 2)

Although levels are still high, there has been a significant fall in the proportion of VIWs reporting anxiety or distress from 77 per cent in phase 1 to 70 per cent in phase 2. Of particular note is the fall in the proportion stating that the court environment had caused them anxiety: in phase 1 over a quarter (27%) said that this had made them anxious, while in phase 2 only one in six said that this had been the case.

The pattern of subgroup differentials is similar in both phase 1 and phase 2. Women were more likely to experience anxiety overall (74% compared with 62% men in phase 2), as were adults (78%) compared with child witnesses (58%), Crown Courts (76%) compared with magistrate's court witnesses (65%), and victims (74%) compared with other prosecution witnesses (63%). Anxiety was especially high among victims of sexual offences (75%) and those affected by intimidation (81%).

In phase 2, VIWs using special measures were less likely than those not using special measures to feel anxious or distressed overall (63% compared with 73%), although there was no difference in the proportion of these subgroups experiencing distress inside the court (both 17%).

In phase 2, as in phase 1, VIWs who did not report anxiety were far more likely to be satisfied with their overall experience (90% compared with 54% of those reporting anxiety as a result of the whole experience).

There have been significant reductions in all subgroups for both overall levels of anxiety and anxiety caused by the courtroom environment. More detailed analysis shows that the reduction in anxiety caused by the court environment is evident across all subgroups, indicating that the reduction is genuine, rather than simply a result of changes in the profile of VIWs between surveys. Figure 7.2 displays the full details.

Although women and victims of sex offences were more likely than average to feel anxious overall, it is interesting to note that these subgroups were slightly less likely than average to feel anxious as a result of the court environment, and this pattern is evident in both survey years. This suggests that although these types of witness are particularly prone to be distressed, measures put in place in court to help these witnesses are effective in ensuring that stress is minimised during this part of their experience.

As noted above, there has been a reduction across all subgroups in the proportion of VIWs experiencing stress as a result of their court experiences. The level of anxiety induced by the court has fallen particularly for the following subgroups: men (from 32% in phase 1 to 18%), child witnesses (from 28% to 16%), Crown Court witnesses (from 28% to 15%), and for victims of sexual offences (from 22% to 12%).

Figure 7.2:   Anxiety as a result of court environment by various subgroups (phase 1 and 2)

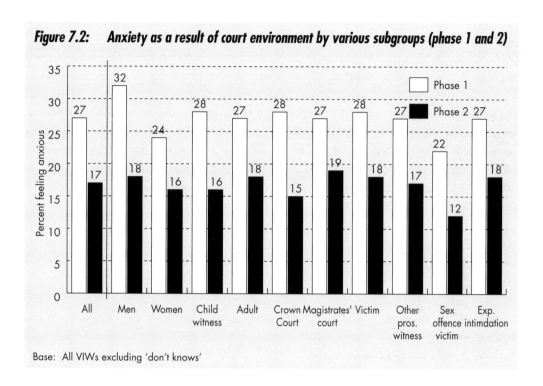

Base: All VIWs excluding 'don't knows'

What made VIWs feel anxious or distressed

All VIWs who said the experience or the court environment had made them feel anxious or distressed were asked, unprompted, what had made them feel like this. VIWs were able to mention more than one cause. The most commonly reported causes of anxiety in phase 2 (as in phase 1) concerned the defendant and his or her friends or family. Twenty-four per cent mentioned seeing the defendant in court, seven per cent the prospect of having to see the defendant afterwards if he or she was acquitted, and six per cent seeing friends or family of the defendant. Other concerns included:

- not knowing what would happen (17%)

- giving evidence and speaking in front of the court (14%)

- exacerbating stress/effect on mental health (11%)

- the defence lawyer (6%)

- reliving experiences or having the past dragged up in court (7%).

Discrimination

All VIWs were asked if they felt that anyone had discriminated against them (described as treating them "differently or unfairly") at any stage in the process of being a witness. In phase 2, fourteen per cent of VIWs felt they had been discriminated against in some way (no change from 15% in phase 1). Of course it is possible that in some cases these perceptions were unfair or mistaken, so this may overestimate the real level of discrimination. Equally it may be that some instances of discrimination may have gone unnoticed, which may possibly tend to counterbalance any overestimation. However, it may be argued that whether or not discrimination occurred, it is VIWs' perception that is important and influences their level of satisfaction. Most (71%) of those who reported discrimination were dissatisfied with their experience, compared with only 25 per cent of those who did not report discrimination.

The vast majority (78%) of those who had experienced discrimination said that it occurred at court; 33 per cent said that it happened before court, while ten per cent said they were discriminated against after court[40].

Table 7.1:   Causes of discrimination (phase 2)

Base: All who felt discriminated against (78)	%
Defence lawyer	45
Police	35
CPS/ lawyers	17
Judge/ magistrate	13
Court staff	4

Table 7.1 shows that most reported discrimination was perceived as coming from defence lawyers (45%). This seems unsurprising, given that most of the sample were prosecution witnesses, and that defence lawyers can be expected to use any permissible tactic available to them during cross-examination. More surprisingly perhaps, 35 per cent said that they had been discriminated against by the police. Seventeen per cent said they felt discriminated against by the CPS lawyer and 13 per cent said they felt discriminated against by the judge or magistrate.

---

40 These percentages add to more than 100 per cent as discrimination could have occurred at more than one stage.

In phase 2 compared with phase 1, a higher proportion of VIWs said they had been discriminated against by the police (35% compared with 20% of all VIWs feeling they had suffered discrimination).

VIWs were also asked in what way they felt they were treated differently or unfairly.

Table 7.2: Forms of discrimination (phase 2)

Base: All who felt discriminated against (78)	%
Made to feel at fault/ in the wrong	21
Not given enough support	21
Defendant treated as more important/better	13
Not given enough opportunity to speak	10
Not given enough information	9
Accused of lying	8

Table 7.2 shows that the most common way in which VIWs felt discriminated against in phase 2 was being made to feel they were at fault or in the wrong (mentioned by 21% of VIWs who felt discriminated against). Thirteen per cent felt that the defendant's rights had been put before theirs, while ten per cent said they were not given enough opportunity to speak when giving evidence. Some of these reasons suggest that they were not treated differently because they had particular characteristics, or were members of a particular group, but were complaining about insensitive treatment. Without further information it is difficult to tell whether these examples are really indicative of discrimination, or simply reflect the adversarial nature of the CJS.

Twenty-one percent of VIWs who felt discriminated against said that this was because they had been treated unfairly by not being given enough support. This is also difficult to take at face value, because it is not known what they meant by "enough support". On the one hand, vulnerable witnesses may need additional support to place them on an equal footing, but on the other, consideration needs to be given to the defendant's rights.

Satisfaction

VIWs were asked to rate their level of satisfaction with the way they were treated by the following: CPS lawyer; defence lawyer; court staff; Victim Support; the Witness Service and judge/magistrate. After being asked about satisfaction with individual agencies, VIWs were asked to rate their overall satisfaction with the experience of being a witness. VIWs were asked to rate each agency/individual on a four-point scale. Table 7.3 gives the detailed findings for the two survey phases, while Figure 7.3 summarises these results, showing the overall level of satisfaction and dissatisfaction. A more detailed discussion of the results for each agency are given in the sections which follow.

Table 7.3:   VIWs' satisfaction with their treatment by CJS agencies (phase 1 and 2)

	Phase	Base*	Satisfaction rating			
			Very satisfied (%)	Fairly satisfied (%)	Fairly dissatisfied (%)	Very dissatisfied (%)
Police	1	540	52	28	10	10
	2	546	53	29	9	8
CPS/prosecution	1	369	54	26	8	12
lawyer	2	343	51	31	9	8
Defence lawyer	1	338	14	31	20	35
	2	302	10	24	21	45
Court staff	1	525	72	23	3	2
	2	540	71	26	2	1
Victim Support	1	196	65	24	6	5
	2	184	65	22	8	5
Witness Service	1	463	81	15	3	1
	2	495	84	15	1	*
Judge/magistrate	1	359	65	27	4	3
	2	332	61	31	4	3
Overall	1	538	21	43	14	22
	2	561	26	43	14	17

* (1) Bases are all VIWs in contact with each organisation excluding 'don't knows'; (2) for court staff, the level of 'don't knows' was five per cent in both surveys; and (3) for Victim Support, the level of 'don't knows' was very high in both surveys – 13 per cent in phase 1, and 15 per cent in phase 2.

The summary results shown in Figure 7.3 indicate that in both survey years, satisfaction was highest for court staff, the Witness Service and the judge or magistrate, and lowest for the defence lawyer. Mostly, results were very similar for the two survey years, although there has been a significant fall in the proportion satisfied with the defence lawyer (from 45% to 34%) and a small but significant increase in the proportion satisfied with the Witness

Service (from 96% to 99%). There has been an encouraging increase (statistically significant at 10% level) in overall satisfaction from 64% to 69%.

Changes in satisfaction scores should be viewed in the context of changes in the sample profile between years. As detailed in Chapter 1, the principal differences between the two survey samples is an increase in the proportion of child witnesses in phase 2 compared with phase 1 (42% compared with 34%) and an increase in the proportion of magistrates' court witnesses (from 38% to 57%). This is discussed further in the following sections, which give detailed accounts of the satisfaction scores for each agency.

Figure 7.3: Summary of satisfaction with CJS agencies/individuals (phase 1 and 2)

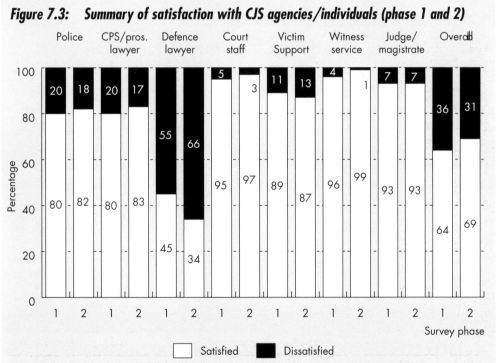

Base: All VIWs having contact with each, excluding 'don't knows'. Base sizes for phase 2 data vary from n=184 (Victim support) to n=561 (overall satisfaction). Base sizes were similar in phase 1

Note: Percentage of don't knows ranged from zero to five per cent in phase 2, except for Victim Support where 15 per cent gave a don't know response

Satisfaction with the police

Most VIWs (80% in phase 1, 82% in phase 2) were satisfied with the way the police treated them, with 53 per cent in phase 2 saying they were 'very satisfied'. This compares to 89 per cent satisfied and 60 per cent 'very satisfied' in the Witness Satisfaction Survey of 2002 (WSS 2002).

Victims of sexual offences were particularly likely to be satisfied with their treatment by the police (90% satisfied in both survey years). This seems surprising, given past criticisms in the research literature about the treatment of victims of sex offences by the police (see Home Office 1998, Annex A, for a review of the literature). However attrition is high in these cases, so those cases which reach court may not be typical. It is suspected that those victims whose cases who do not reach court may be more critical.

The high rate of satisfaction among child witnesses (89% satisfied in phase 1, 87% in phase 2) seems less surprising, given evidence from both this survey and the WSS 2002 that child witnesses tend to be more satisfied overall. Similarly, the finding that witnesses who experienced intimidation had a lower satisfaction level with the police (69% satisfied in phase 1, 75% in phase 2[41]) seems unsurprising in the light of the evidence in Chapter 2 that most witnesses who experienced intimidation before court did not feel that it was dealt with effectively. Witnesses who only feared intimidation had a similar satisfaction level to those who did not fear or experience intimidation (90% compared with 92%).

In most cases the police will be the first point of contact a witness has with the CJS, so it seems unsurprising that satisfaction with the police was associated with overall satisfaction. Eight in ten (78%) of VIWs in phase 2 who were satisfied with the police were also satisfied with their overall experience of being a witness.

There has been a two percentage point increase in satisfaction with the police between the two survey years. The small (non-significant) increase may be partly attributable to the increase in the representation of magistrates' court witnesses in phase 2 as satisfaction with the police has increased slightly within this subgroup (from 77% to 83%[42]) with no corresponding increase in the satisfaction scores of Crown Court witnesses.

---

41 Difference between two survey years not significant.
42 Not significant.

Satisfaction with CPS lawyer

All VIWs who had contact with the lawyer for the CPS were asked how satisfied they had been with the way this lawyer treated them. Satisfaction with the CPS lawyer was also high (80% in phase 1, 83% in phase 2). This compares to 87 per cent in the WSS 2002.

Again, child witnesses had a higher level of satisfaction with their treatment by the CPS lawyer than adults (90% satisfied compared to 77% in phase 2). Witnesses who experienced intimidation were less satisfied (77% in phase 2) than both witnesses who feared intimidation (91%) and those who neither feared or experienced intimidation (89%). Possibly, witnesses who experienced intimidation may have blamed the CPS lawyer for failing to protect them, or failing to respond to intimidation, despite the fact that most intimidation was said to have occurred before court or afterwards (see Chapter 2).

Victims tended to be less satisfied than other prosecution witnesses (80% compared to 88%). One reason might be that they had higher expectations of the CPS lawyer, in particular to represent them, rather than the Crown[43]. Satisfaction with the CPS lawyer was associated with overall satisfaction: 76 per cent of those satisfied with the CPS were satisfied with their overall experience.

Satisfaction with the CPS/prosecution lawyer has risen by three percentage points since phase 1. This small (non-significant) increase does not appear to be attributable to an increase in satisfaction within any particular subgroup, more an overall slight increase across most subgroups.

Satisfaction with defence lawyer

VIWs were least satisfied with defence lawyers, and the level of dissatisfaction has increased further since phase 1. In phase 2, 66 per cent of VIWs in contact with a defence lawyer were dissatisfied (45% "very dissatisfied"). This has increased from 55 per cent in phase 1, as shown in Figure 7.4. This compares with only 35 per cent dissatisfied in the WSS 2002, although this may reflect the higher proportion of defence witnesses interviewed in the latter survey.

In Chapter 4, VIWs' perceptions of their treatment by the defence lawyer are described in more detail, and show that prosecution witnesses in phase 2 were more likely than in phase 1 to consider the defence lawyer to lack courtesy towards them and to not give them adequate opportunity to ask questions. These findings therefore help explain the fall in satisfaction ratings.

---

43 The role of the victim in the CJS was one of the subjects in a recent consultation paper, Home Office 2001.

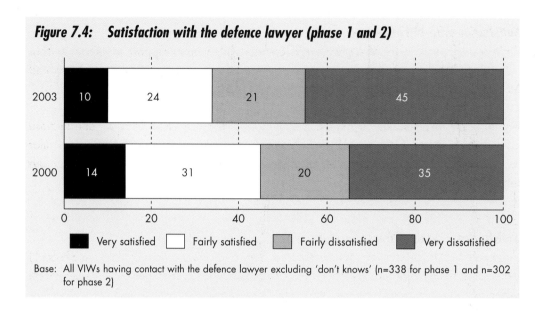

Figure 7.4: *Satisfaction with the defence lawyer (phase 1 and 2)*

| | Very satisfied | Fairly satisfied | Fairly dissatisfied | Very dissatisfied |

2003: 10 | 24 | 21 | 45
2000: 14 | 31 | 20 | 35

Base: All VIWs having contact with the defence lawyer excluding 'don't knows' (n=338 for phase 1 and n=302 for phase 2)

Male VIWs were more likely than female VIWs to be satisfied with the defence lawyer's treatment of them (40% compared with 30% in phase 2). Victims tended to be less satisfied than other prosecution witnesses (31% compared with 38%), and victims of sex offences were slightly less likely than average to be satisfied (27% satisfied)[44]. Satisfaction with the defence lawyer was associated with overall satisfaction: 90 per cent of VIWs who were satisfied with their treatment by the defence lawyer were satisfied overall.

The overall decrease in satisfaction does not appear to be linked to any particular subgroup, with decreases occurring consistently across most subgroups. However, there has been a particularly noticeable decrease in satisfaction with the defence lawyer among other (non-victim) prosecution witnesses with 54 per cent expressing satisfaction in phase 1, this falling to 38 per cent in phase 2.

Satisfaction with court staff

Satisfaction with court staff was high, with most VIWs (95% in phase 1, 97% in phase 2) saying they were satisfied, and many (71% in phase 2) saying they were very satisfied.

Satisfaction is very high (over 90%) across the board, and there are no significant changes by year.

---

44 None of the differences quoted earlier in this paragraph are significant.

Satisfaction with Victim Support

Eighty-seven per cent of VIWs who had contact with Victim Support in phase 2 were satisfied with the way they were treated. Only thirteen per cent said they were dissatisfied (no change since phase 1).

However, only 38 per cent of VIWs said they had contact with Victim Support, and of those a significant minority (15%) were unable to express a view on their treatment – this is similar to the rate of contact in phase 1. The smaller sub-bases in both surveys makes it more difficult to draw general conclusions.

Satisfaction with the Witness Service

Virtually all VIWs in contact with the Witness Service (99% in phase 2, 96% in phase 1) were satisfied with the way in which the Witness Service treated them, with a very high proportion (84% in phase 2) saying they were 'very satisfied'.

The small but significant increase in the proportion satisfied with the Witness Service is reflected across most subgroups, although there was a more marked increase among Crown Court witnesses (from 94% to 99%) and among those who experienced intimidation (from 94% to 98%).

Satisfaction with judge/magistrate

All VIWs who gave evidence were asked how satisfied they were with the way in which the judge or magistrate spoke to them. The vast majority of VIWs (93% in both years) were satisfied with their treatment, and many (61% in phase 2) said they were 'very satisfied'.

Seventy per cent of VIWs who were satisfied with their treatment by the judge or magistrate were satisfied with their overall experience: only 30 per cent of those who were dissatisfied with the judge/magistrate were satisfied with their overall treatment.

Overall satisfaction with the experience of being a witness

All VIWs were asked if they were satisfied with their experience overall as a witness. As with the phase 1 survey and the WSS 2002, satisfaction was higher with individual agencies than overall (for a discussion of the reasons for this see Whitehead, 2000). Sixty-nine per cent of VIWs said that they were satisfied overall with their experience, with 26 per cent saying they were 'very satisfied'.

Figure 7.5 compares overall satisfaction in both survey years as well as with the WSS 2002. Satisfaction has increased by five percentage points between phase 1 and phase 2, although this change is not significant. There has, however, been a significant decrease in the proportion of VIWs stating that they were "very dissatisfied" overall, from 22 per cent to 17 per cent. These changes are very encouraging indicators of improved service pre- and post-implementation of measures.

Figure 7.5:   *Overall satisfaction with service (phase 1, 2 and WSS 2002)*

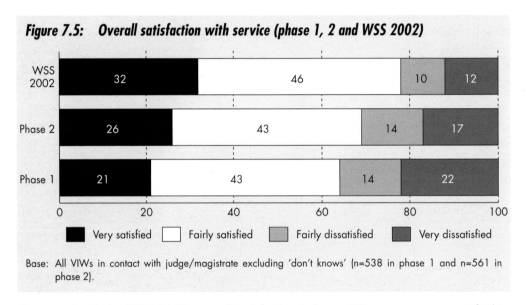

Base: All VIWs in contact with judge/magistrate excluding 'don't knows' (n=538 in phase 1 and n=561 in phase 2).

Compared with the WSS 2002, overall satisfaction is lower (78 per cent were satisfied in the WSS 2002, and 32 per cent 'very satisfied'). This mirrors a similar differential between the phase 1 survey and the WSS phase 1.

Table 7.4 shows how overall satisfaction varies according to the characteristics of the witness in both survey years. A significant change between phase 1 and phase 2 within any subgroup is indicated.

There were similar differences between sub-groups in phases 1 and 2. Thus, child witnesses had a significantly higher level of satisfaction with their overall experience, with 76 per cent saying they were satisfied, compared with 64 per cent of adult witnesses. Satisfaction was also higher among male compared with female VIWs (72% and 67%), and among witnesses at magistrates' courts compared with those at Crown Courts (71% compared with 66%)[45].

---

45 Neither of these differences significant.

Table 7.4: *Overall satisfaction with the CJS (percentage very/fairly satisfied) and percentage point change between phases 1 and 2*

Base: All VIWs excluding 'don't knows'	Overall satisfaction (%)		Change from phase 1 to phase 2 (percentage points)
	Phase 1 (n=538)	Phase 2 (n=561)	
Witness type			
Victim	61	67	+6**
Other prosecution	67	71	+4
Court type			
Crown	60	66	+6
Magistrate	67	71	+4
Sex			
Male	69	72	+3
Female	59	67	+8
Age			
Under 17	73	76	+3
17 or over	59	64	+5
Intimidated			
Experienced	48	59	+11*
Feared	66	80	+14*
Any intimidation	57	64	+7*
Neither feared/experienced	78	81	+3
Offence			
Sexual	66	67	+1
Other	63	69	+6*
Use of special measures			
Yes	N/A	76	
No		65	
Total	64	69	+5**

* denotes significant difference from Phase 1, p<0.05
** denotes significant different from phase 1, p<0.10.

Victims were less likely to say they were satisfied with their experience as a witness (67% compared with 71% of other prosecution witnesses). This finding was significant at the 10 per cent level.

Experience of intimidation was strongly related to overall satisfaction, with only 59 per cent of those who experienced intimidation saying they were satisfied, compared with 81 per cent of those who neither experienced nor feared intimidation.

An important finding in phase 2 is that those using special measures were significantly more likely to express overall satisfaction compared with those who did not (76% compared with 65%).

Turning now to changes between the two years, it is first important to note that changes in the sample profile have not had any impact on the increase in satisfaction. There has been an increase of a similar magnitude for both children and adults, and the Crown Court as well as magistrates' courts, the two areas where there has been a change in sample profile. Thus the increase on the total sample is "real" and not simply accounted for by sample changes.

Table 7.4 demonstrates that increases in overall satisfaction are evident in most subgroups. However, a review of the results suggests that increases are more concentrated in particular subgroups:

- Satisfaction has increased among women more than men, but interestingly there has been no change in satisfaction among victims of sex offences, the majority of whom are women.

- There has been no change in the satisfaction levels of witnesses who were not affected by intimidation. However, there were marked increases in satisfaction among those either experiencing intimidation (from 48% to 59%), fearing intimidation (from 66% to 80%) or either of the above (from 57% to 64%). This reflects findings reported elsewhere in this report which have suggested a number of ways in which intimidated witnesses are less unhappy in phase 2 compared with phase 1.

Willingness to be a witness again

VIWs were asked two questions to ascertain their willingness to act as a witness again. The first question, also asked in phase 1 and in the WSS surveys, was:

"If you were asked to be a witness again in a criminal trial, how happy would you be to take part?"

However, it was known from the phase 1 survey that a fairly large proportion of those satisfied with their experience (37%) still said they would not be happy to repeat their experience as a witness. This may be because VIWs, although satisfied with their treatment by the police and courts, may be unhappy to take part as a witness again due to other distressing circumstances regarding the case. Also, although VIWs might say that they would be "unhappy" to take on this role again, this does not mean that they would not do it if they were asked. To address these issues, an additional (new) question was asked in phase 2:

"If you were asked to be witness again, how likely would you be to take part?

A minority (44%) of VIWs said they would be happy to be a witness again. Fifty-six per cent said they would not be happy, with 30 per cent saying they would 'not be at all happy'. These figures are virtually unchanged from phase 1. This indicates that although there has been some increase in overall satisfaction, this has not translated into an increase in happiness to repeat their experience. However, despite this there is a clear correlation between overall satisfaction in phase 2 and willingness to be a witness again, with 56 per cent satisfied overall saying that they would happy to do it again compared with just 16 per cent of those dissatisfied. However, this leaves 44 per cent of VIWs who were satisfied with their experience but still unhappy to repeat it, which equates to 30 per cent of all VIWs. The association between these two factors is shown in Figure 7.6. This also shows that one in four in all VIWs were both dissatisfied and unhappy to be a witness again.

A higher proportion of VIWs said they were "likely to agree" to be a witness again than were "happy" to do this. Overall 61 per cent said that they were likely to agree, 27 per cent "very likely". Two in five (39%) said that they would be unlikely to agree[46]. Three in ten (31%) of those who said they would unhappy to be a witness again were nevertheless likely to agree to do it if they were asked. This demonstrates that this second measure is a better predictor of actual likelihood to be a witness again.

Women were more likely than men to say they would repeat their experience (65% compared with 59%), although only 54 per cent of sex offence victims said this. Also, a higher proportion of child (65%) than adult witnesses (58%) said that they would be likely to act as a witness again[47]. Experience of intimidation was strongly associated with a lower likelihood to agree again (50%); this compares with 74 per cent of those neither fearing nor experiencing intimidation.

---

46 These figures exclude the five per cent who said that they did not know if they would be likely to or not.
47 Not significant.

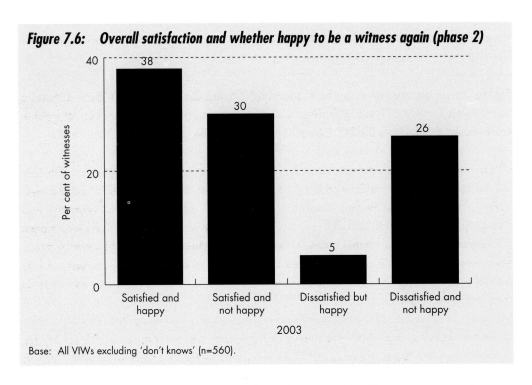

Figure 7.6: Overall satisfaction and whether happy to be a witness again (phase 2)

Base: All VIWs excluding 'don't knows' (n=560).

There is a strong correlation between overall satisfaction and likelihood to agree to being a witness again, with 70 per cent of those satisfied saying they would be likely to agreee compared with only 33 per cent of those dissatisfied.

Confidence in the Criminal Justice System

All VIWs were asked how confident they were that the criminal justice system:

- is effective in bringing people who commit crimes to justice;

- meets the needs of victims of crime;

- respects the rights of people accused of committing crime and treats them fairly;

- deals with cases promptly and efficiently;

- treats all witnesses fairly and with respect; and also

- how confident they were that the sentences passed by courts are appropriate (new for phase 2).

The first four questions have also been used in the British Crime Surveys (BCS) and Witness Satisfaction Surveys. Figure 7.7 displays the results for both survey phases, alongside comparative figures from the 2002/3 BCS where available.

VIWs in phase 2 were least confident that the courts pass appropriate sentences with only 34 per cent expressing confidence in this (Figure 7.7). For questions asked in both surveys, VIWs in both years were least confident that the CJS deals with cases promptly and efficiently. However, confidence levels were nearly as low in relation to the CJS performance in bringing people who commit crimes to justice and meeting the needs of victims of crime. A larger proportion of VIWs felt confident that the rights of the accused were respected by the CJS and that they were treated fairly than were confident that the CJS treats all witnesses fairly and with respect.

There has been a small but consistent trend between the two phases of the survey for confidence to increase, although only the increase in the proportion of VIWs feeling confident that defendants' rights are respected (from 82% to 89%) is significant.

Compared with the views of the general public as measured by the BCS figures, VIWs in phase 2 were more positive about CJS, being more likely to feel confident that the CJS is effective in bringing criminals to justice; meets the needs of victims; respects the rights of defendants; and deals with cases promptly. This is a very positive finding as it indicates that those actually having experience of the CJS in these contexts have more confidence in the CJS than members of the public in general, most of whom will have had no such experience.

Figure 7.7: Confidence in the CJS (phase 1 and 2 and comparative figures from BCS 2002/3)

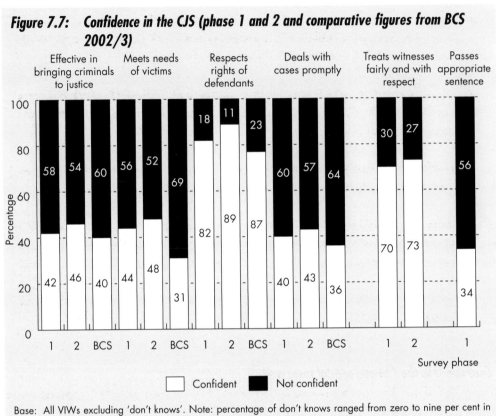

Base: All VIWs excluding 'don't knows'. Note: percentage of don't knows ranged from zero to nine per cent in phase 2. BCS survey: all respondents (general public) 2002/3

Correlates of confidence

There was a consistent pattern in that some groups of VIWs were more confident about each of these aspects of the CJS compared with others. However, this precludes confidence in the rights of defendants, where confidence levels remained uniform across all witness subgroups. However, for all other statements which were more focused on the rights of witnesses and victims, there was a consistent trend in phase 2 with some groups expressing more confidence in the CJS than others[48]:

- *men more than women* (e.g., 54% of men were confident that the CJS meets the needs of victims compared with 44% of women);

---

48 The pattern of differentials was similar in both survey years.

- *magistrates' court more than Crown Court witnesses* (e.g., 39% of magistrate court witnesses were confident that sentences passed by courts were appropriate compared with 27% of Crown Court witnesses);

- *other prosecution witnesses more than victims* (e.g., only 42% of victims were confident that the CJS is effective in bringing people who commit crimes to justice compared with 52 % of other prosecution witnesses);

- *children more than adults* (e.g., 83% of child witnesses were confident that they were treated fairly and with respect compared with 65% of adult witnesses);

- *those not affected by intimidation more than those experiencing it* (e.g., only 39% of intimidated witnesses were confident that the CJS was effective in bringing criminals to justice compared with 55% of those not affected by intimidation); and

- *witnesses receiving special measures compared with those not receiving them* (see below).

Confidence in the CJS and special measures

Figure 7.8 shows how confidence varies according to whether or not VIWs received any of the special measures (phase 2 data).

This shows that VIWs using special measures were more confident that the CJS was effective in bringing those who commit crimes to justice and meets the needs of victims. There were similar (although non-significant) differentials on other measures, and of particular interest is the finding that VIWs using special measures were more likely to consider that witnesses were treated fairly and with respect.

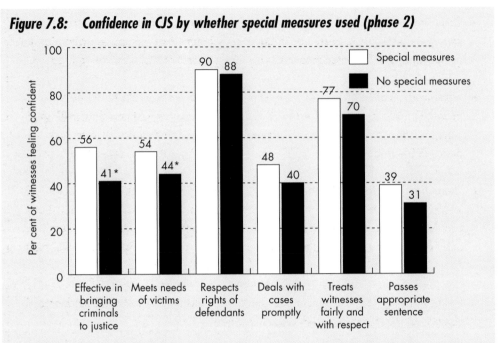

Figure 7.8: Confidence in CJS by whether special measures used (phase 2)

Base: All VIWs excluding 'don't knows'. Note: Percentage of don't knows ranged from zero to nine per cent. * denotes significant at five per cent.

Key points

- Most vulnerable victims and witnesses found their experience stressful, although there was a reduction in these feelings between phases 1 and 2, both overall (from 77% to 70%) and specifically relating to the court environment (from 27% to 17%). VIWs using special measures in phase 2 were less likely than those not using measures to experience anxiety.

- The most commonly reported causes of anxiety were seeing the defendant in court, (mentioned by 24%) and not knowing what would happen (mentioned by 17%).

- 14 per cent of VIW felt they had been discriminated against in some way, most commonly at court; 71 per cent of those who felt discriminated against were dissatisfied with their experience. The most frequently cited cause of discrimination was the defence lawyer (45%).

- Compared with phase 1, VIWs in phase 2 who had contact with a defence lawyer were less likely to express satisfaction with them (34% compared with 45%). Satisfaction with the defence lawyer was highly correlated with overall satisfaction.

- Satisfaction was very high for the Witness Service (96% in phase 1 and 99% in phase 2), judges and magistrates (93% in both years), and the police (80% and 82%). Victims of sexual offences were particularly likely to be satisfied with the police (90% in both years).

- There has been a small (significant at 10% level) increase in the proportion of VIWs who said that they were satisfied overall with their experience, from 64 per cent to 69 per cent. This compares with 78 per cent in the WSS 2002. There has been a corresponding (significant) decrease in the proportion expressing that they were "very dissatisfied" overall, from 22 per cent to 17 per cent.

- In phase 2, VIWs using special measures were more likely to be satisfied overall compared with those not using these measures.

- Overall satisfaction has increased mostly among women and intimidated witnesses.

- Dissatisfaction was strongly associated with whether witnesses felt intimidated.

- 61 per cent of VIWs said that if they were asked to be a witness again, they would be likely to agree to this. However, only 44 per cent of VIWs said they would be "happy" to be a witness again.

- There was a strong correlation between overall satisfaction and likelihood to agree to being a witness again, with 70 per cent of those satisfied saying they would be likely compared with only 33 per cent of those dissatisfied.

- VIWs were most confident that the CJS respects the rights of people accused of committing crime and treats them fairly (89% in phase 2), and least confident that the courts pass appropriate sentences (34%).

- VIWs receiving special measures were more likely to consider that the CJS meets the needs of victims, is effective in bringing criminals to justice and treats witnesses fairly and with respect.

8   Predicting satisfaction and willingness to be a witness again

Understanding witness satisfaction is complex. This report so far has highlighted particular aspects of being a witness that are clear sources of satisfaction and dissatisfaction for witnesses. However, looking at individual statements in isolation can potentially lead to an unbalanced view of witness priorities. A "key driver" model was therefore developed based on the principles of multivariate analysis.

The approach taken here was to build a model that could predict the key drivers of:

- overall satisfaction;
- willingness to be a witness again; and
- likelihood to agree to be a witness again.

The theory is relatively simple, namely that witnesses' level of overall satisfaction (or willingness to be a witness again, or likelihood to be a witness again) is a result of how they perceive the many different aspects or elements of their experience. In other words, there is one consequence (say satisfaction) and many causes (different aspects of the experience of being a witness). The aim of the multivariate analysis is to find the best way of predicting the consequence (called the 'dependent variable') from the optimum combination of the many different causes (called the 'independent variables').

The approach taken was first to consider all possible factors. Any variables with large amounts of missing data were removed. Logistic regression was then carried out for each of the three dependent variables mentioned above.

Variables were not included in the regression if the number of respondents answering the question was less than 100.

The number of factors was then reduced further by consideration of two issues. First, consideration was given to the likelihood that there was a high degree of association between factors since they were essentially measuring the same thing, or were due to the dependent variable (e.g. was confidence with the CJS likely to be influenced by the experience of being a witness, rather than contributing to overall satisfaction). Second, the factors were examined to determine which were adding little to the accuracy of the model.

The final models include only those factors most strongly correlated with the dependent variable, which were considered not too strongly interrelated to the dependent variable to include in the model.

Regressions on overall satisfaction

The strongest predictors of overall satisfaction among all vulnerable and intimidated witnesses were their satisfaction with the police and their perception of whether the CJS meets the needs of victims. Other predictors included respondents' satisfaction with the defence lawyer and the extent to which they felt they were able to give their evidence accurately.

Table 8.1 lists the key variables that affected overall satisfaction. The first column lists the correlation coefficients each of the variables had with overall satisfaction. The second column shows the number of respondents who answered each question.

The third column, shows the regression betas which ranged from zero to one (or -1 if the relationship was a negative one). Compared to the correlation coefficients (which are a measure of one-to-one association), regression betas give the relative importance of each variable in predicting overall satisfaction after allowing for the effects of the other variables. Those betas furthest from zero become the largest key drivers.

The accuracy of the regression on overall satisfaction was 53 per cent, a very satisfactory figure for satisfaction modelling.

Table 8.1: Multiple regression on overall satisfaction

	Correlation	Number of respondents answering	Regression Beta
$R^2 =$			0.53
Were you satisfied or dissatisfied with your treatment as a witness in this case by the police?	0.50	538	0.21
How confident are you that the Criminal Justice System meets the needs of victims of crime?	0.54	538	0.21
Were you satisfied or dissatisfied with your treatment, as a witness in this case, by the defence lawyer?	0.47	300	0.13
Did you feel you were able to give your evidence accurately?	0.42	341	0.13
How confident are you that the criminal justice system treats all witnesses fairly and with respect?	0.56	546	0.11
Was there any point in the whole process when you felt really anxious or distressed, either by the whole experience of being a witness or by the court environment?	0.33	561	0.11
Were you satisfied or dissatisfied with your treatment, as a witness in this case, by the prosecution lawyer and the Crown Prosecution Service?	0.49	340	0.09
Were you given any information about what would happen in court?	0.33	561	0.08
Did you feel that your feelings of being intimidated or threatened while you were at court were dealt with effectively?	0.43	180	0.07
How helpful would you have found the use of screens in the courtroom?	-0.32	177	0.07
Did you feel you needed help of any kind before you left the court?	-0.52	149	-0.07
Did you feel you were discriminated against at any point during this case, either before you went to court, while at court or afterwards?	-0.36	559	-0.07
What effect, if any, did the change in date have on the way you felt about going to court?	-0.40	109	-0.06

Regressions on willingness to be a witness again

Multiple regression analysis was used to predict the key drivers of witnesses' willingness to be a witness again.

Table 8.2 shows the relative correlation coefficients and regression betas.

Table 8.2: **_Multiple regression on willingness to be a witness again_**

	Correlation	Base	Regression Beta
$R^2 =$			0.29
Were you satisfied or dissatisfied with your experience overall as a witness in this case?	0.48	552	0.29
Was there any point in the whole process when you felt really anxious or distressed, either by the whole experience of being a witness or by the court environment?	0.35	560	0.18
Were you satisfied or dissatisfied with your treatment, as a witness in this case, by the defence lawyer?	0.38	297	0.12
How confident are you that the Criminal Justice System meets the needs of victims of crime?	0.35	537	0.10
What effect, if any, did the change in date have on the way you felt about going to court?	-0.46	111	-0.10
How helpful would you have found it to give evidence using a video link instead of in the courtroom?	0.33	201	-0.07

The first point to note is that compared to the analysis of the drivers of overall satisfaction there were fewer high correlations, giving a smaller R2 and fewer key drivers in the final equation.

This is not an uncommon finding in multivariate analysis where it is generally more difficult to predict actual behaviour than attitudes. Future behaviour is even more difficult to predict as respondents are often less willing to make definite judgements about behaviour which may vary depending on future circumstances such as the severity of the court case for example. An R2 of more than 0.2 is still worth commenting on, but caution is needed when reaching conclusions from this analysis.

Overall satisfaction was by far the main driver. Feeling anxious or distressed by the situation of being a witness was also of high importance, followed by satisfaction with how the defence lawyer treated the respondent and whether respondents believed that the CJS met the needs of victims.

Regressions on agreeing to become a witness in the future

Multiple regression analysis was also used to determine the key drivers of the likelihood of witnesses agreeing to become a witness in the future. This could potentially be subtly different from considering whether respondents would be willing to be a witness again in the future. Results of this analysis can be found in Table 8.3 below.

Table 8.3: Multiple regression on likelihood to agree to be a witness again

	Correlation	Base	Regression Beta
R2 =			0.24
Were you satisfied or dissatisfied with your experience overall as a witness in this case?	0.42	533	0.25
Do you feel that you received enough support from the police when you gave your statement?	0.31	508	0.17
Do you think if these special measures had NOT been available to you, you would still have been willing and able to attend court and give evidence?	0.36	155	0.13
Were you satisfied or dissatisfied with your treatment, as a witness in this case, by the defence lawyer?	0.33	287	0.11
How confident are you that the Criminal Justice System meets the needs of victims of crime?	0.31	519	0.09
What effect, if any, did the change in date have on the way you felt about going to court?	-0.39	106	-0.09

As with the analysis of the drivers of witnesses' willingness to be a witness again there were fewer high correlations giving a smaller R^2.

As previously, overall satisfaction was the key driver. Next in importance was whether or not the respondents felt they got enough support from the police, followed by whether they would still be willing to attend court and give evidence without special measures. As in the previous regression, satisfaction with the defence lawyer was a further middle-level driver.

Although the main driver of satisfaction was the same for these two last regressions analyses, the above analysis shows that there were differences between the drivers of 'willingness to be a witness again' and the drivers of 'likelihood that respondents will agree to be a witness again'.

The survey of vulnerable and intimidated witnesses (VIWs) project is part of a wider programme of research evaluating the implementation and effectiveness of measures to assist VIWs in court. The aims of the VIW survey were to determine (a) to what extent the measures have been successful in helping VIWs give best evidence and (b) to what extent the measures have improved the satisfaction of VIWs with their treatment by the criminal justice system. The extent to which the measures have been successful in these respects has direct relevance to two key Home Office and CJS Public Service Agreement (PSA) targets. The first of these (the 'Justice Gap PSA') is to increase the number of crimes for which an offender is brought to justice and reduce ineffective trials[49]. The second ('the 'Confidence PSA') is to improve public confidence in the CJS and satisfaction of victims and witnesses[50] (http://www.homeoffice.gov.uk/docs/psa02_ch6.pdf).

The special measures already in place are:

- In the Crown Court: screening witness from the accused, evidence by live link, removal of wigs and gowns (Crown Court measure only) evidence given in private and aids to communication (the last measure is available to vulnerable witnesses only).
- In Crown Court, for vulnerable witnesses but not intimidated witnesses: video-recorded evidence-in-chief.
- In magistrates' courts (including Youth Court) for child witnesses in need of special protection only: evidence by live link and video recorded evidence-in-chief.

Many of the measures therefore remain to be implemented in the magistrates' courts, while their wider extension to intimidated witnesses in the Crown Court is also awaited.

This final chapter will help to inform the decision about wider implementation by drawing together the evidence about the effectiveness of special measures and their potential to impact upon the two PSA Targets previously mentioned.

---

49 Home Office PSA Target 3/CJS PSA Target 2 is 'To improve the delivery of justice by increasing the number of crimes for which an offender is brought to justice to 1.2 million by 2005-6; with an improvement in all CJS areas, a greater increase in the worse performing areas and a reduction in the proportion of ineffective trials'.

50 Home Office PSA Target 4/CJS PSA Target 3 is 'To improve the level of public confidence in the Criminal Justice System, including increasing that of ethnic minority communities, and increasing year on year the satisfaction of victims and witnesses, whilst respecting the rights of defendants'.

Main conclusions

Special measures beneficial for VIWs' well-being. VIWs who used special measures were less likely than those not using special measures to feel anxious or distressed overall.

Special measures beneficial for VIWs' evidence. VIWs who used special measures were (slightly) more likely to report that they had been able to give their evidence completely accurately.

Special measures which made it possible for the VIW to give evidence. In addition, a third of VIWs who used special measures said they would not have been willing and able to give evidence if these measures had not been available to them. This finding is very important in relation to the 'Justice Gap' PSA, in that it suggests that there is a proportion of cases involving VIWs which are now resulting in offenders being brought to justice where, formerly, this would not have occurred.

All special measures viewed favourably. The vast majority of VIWs found it helpful to have had a live TV link, screens, video recorded evidence-in-chief, clearing of the public gallery (giving evidence in private) or the removal of wigs and gowns. The value of special measures is further demonstrated by the extensive level of demand for measures among VIWs who were not given access to them.

Increased satisfaction among VIWs who used special measures. VIWs who used special measures were significantly more likely to express overall satisfaction with the criminal justice system, compared with those who did not use special measures.

VIWs less satisfied than general victims and witnesses. When the VIW survey findings were compared with those for the Witness Satisfaction Surveys, VIWs were found to be less satisfied with their experience of the CJS than general victims and witnesses, although phase 2 showed an improvement on the phase 1 figures.

An association between special measures and confidence. VIWs using special measures were more confident that the CJS was effective in bringing those who commit crimes to justice and meeting the needs of victims than those who did not use special measures. Also, VIWs who used special measures were more likely to consider themselves to have been treated fairly and with respect than those who did not use special measures.

Indicators of satisfaction. Key predictors of overall satisfaction included feeling satisfied with the police, feeling satisfied with the defence lawyer, feeling able to give their evidence accurately, and lack of feelings of anxiety or distress. Witness satisfaction was also strongly associated with intimidation, the verdict, court facilities and satisfaction with how much information they received.

VIWs willingness to be a witness again. Less than half of VIWs said they would be happy to be a witness again, although it is encouraging that almost two-thirds said they would be a witness again if asked. (In the Witness Satisfaction Survey of 2002, 67 per cent would be happy to be a witness again, and 80 per cent would do it again if required.)

Overall, special measures were viewed positively by VIWs. The VIW survey provides convincing evidence that the measures have led to an increase in satisfaction among VIWs, both with the CJS generally and with specific aspects of their experience of giving evidence. There are consequently positive implications for that element of the Confidence PSA which relates to victim and witness satisfaction.

However, there is still more that can be done to meet the needs of VIWs. Although reduced, anxiety levels among VIWs are still high and there is still a fairly wide gap between the satisfaction rating for VIWs and victims and witnesses in general. Of course, we can never hope to make the experience of giving evidence pleasant, but the use of special measures have gone some way towards reducing the stressfulness of the experience, though can never remove it altogether. The differences between phase 1 and phase 2 of the survey research show how the further implementation of special measures will help improve satisfaction – and further help to raise confidence in the CJS more generally – and bring more offences to justice. The surveys also show that there is more demand for the use of special measures.

Finally, the findings strongly suggest that special measures should be implemented more widely – e.g., in the magistrates' courts – for the benefit of VIWs and therefore justice. Although the cases heard in magistrates' courts involve less serious offences than in Crown Courts, some victims and witnesses will be vulnerable and/or intimidated. Furthermore, it can be argued that any experience of a courtroom, whether in a higher or lower court, is inherently stressful.

Some judges have expressed concerns that evidence given on videotape or via live TV link reduces the immediacy of impact on the court and thus may reduce convictions. However, there is no research evidence to support such concerns. In fact, what the survey findings suggest is that some of the cases now finding their way to court and resulting in conviction might never have reached court before the introduction of special measures, due to witness withdrawal or termination by the CPS due to doubts about how witnesses would perform in open court.

Appendix A   Methodological details

Recruitment of VIWs

The recruitment of witnesses was carried out in the same way in each survey phase. All courts where a Witness Service operated at the time of the phase 1 survey (86 Crown Courts and 94 magistrates' courts) were asked to recruit vulnerable and intimidated witnesses for the survey. Witness Service co-ordinators were invited to briefings given by the members of the Home Office and BMRB research teams to give them a better understanding of the objectives of the research and the recruitment procedures. Full written instructions were also provided. At phase 1, recruitment took place during October-December 2000. At phase 2 the recruitment period was March-May 2003.

At phase 1, 62 Crown Courts and 42 magistrates courts recruited VIWs for the survey. In order to find out why some courts did not help BMRB with the survey, all non-responding courts were approached and asked their reasons. A full analysis of the reasons is given in Appendix B, although the main reasons were either because no VIWs were identified, or because of resource problems – the WS was not yet fully up and running or the WS was under-staffed. In phase 2, the participation rate of courts was much higher – 71 Crown Courts and 67 magistrates' courts became involved. This higher participation rate could be attributed to a number of factors. In many courts the Witness Service was newly set up at the time of the phase 1 survey. However, by phase 2, all Witness Services should have been running for some time and it could be expected that the services were better staffed and more efficiently run. It may also be the case that VIWs were easier to identify in phase 2 due to improved police procedures – this may have reduced the number of courts declining because there were no VIWs identified.

At court, WS representatives were asked to identify and approach all VIWs, and to record some details about the nature of their vulnerabilities. Witnesses were then asked whether they would be willing to be contacted by a BMRB interviewer (for witnesses aged under 17, permission from a parent or guardian was also required). If they agreed to this, then they were asked for some contact details and whether they had any special requirements for the interview (e.g. need of a translator/interpreter).

The WS was asked to recruit witnesses with a number of defined vulnerabilities (see Chapter 1). These were to include both prosecution and defence witnesses (although the

WS has very little contact with the latter so very few were recruited), and to exclude police and expert witnesses. Witnesses who turned up to court but did not give evidence were also to be included.

All VIWs approached were given a copy of a Home Office letter giving information about the survey. Recruitment forms were returned to BMRB in batches throughout the recruitment period.

Before contact details were passed to the fieldforce, all interviewers were police-checked (because the survey involved interviewing children), and attended a briefing given by BMRB. If the witness was a child aged under 14, then the interview was conducted with the parent or other person with parental responsibility. If aged between 14 and 16, then the interviewer had discretion as to whether to interview the child directly or through a proxy parent.

In phase 1, interviews took place during November 2000-February 2001. In phase 2, the fieldwork period was April to June 2003.

Profile of witnesses recruited for the research

Table A.1 shows the profile of all witnesses approached, all witnesses recruited (i.e. agreeing to take part in the survey) and all witnesses interviewed by BMRB at phase 2. It also compares the profile of witnesses interviewed in phase 2 with witnesses interviewed in the earlier phase 1.

Table A.1:   Respondent profile

	All approached by Witness Service*	Phase 2 VIWs recruited*	Interviews achieved+	Phase 1 Interviews achieved+
Base	1,737	793	569	552
	%	%	%	%
Women	59	61	60	57
Aged under 17	41	41	42	34
Victim of sexual offence	19	18	15	16
Racially motivated	7	7	10	8
Feared/suffered intimidation	51	55	70	69
Limiting physical disability	9	12	13	14
Learning disability	4	4	7	5
Mental illness/disorder	3	3		
Likely to be distressed	41	44	45	51
Victim	61	65	62	58
Other prosecution witness	37	34	37	41
Defence witness	2	1	1	2
Crown	55	46	43	62
Magistrates	45	54	57	38
North			35	28
Midlands			31	31
South East			24	20
South West/Wales			10	21

* Data taken from recruitment questionnaire.
\+ Data taken from interview questionnaire.

The figures show that there was relatively little difference between the profile of VIWs recruited and interviewed, and all VIWs approached by the WS. The main differences were:

- victims of sexual offences were slightly less likely to be interviewed, and witnesses with a physical difficulty slightly more likely to be interviewed.

- There was a higher rate of reporting of intimidation among those interviewed than appeared to be the case among all VIWs. However, as discussed further in Chapter 1, this could be party explained by the different ways in which the questions to elicit experience of intimidation were asked at the recruitment and interview stages. However, it may also be that witnesses affected by intimidation were particularly likely to want to participate in the research.

- There was a large difference in the recruitment rate of VIWs at Crown Courts and magistrates' courts. Crown Court witnesses were significantly less likely to agree to participate compared with magistrates' court witnesses, and therefore their presence is somewhat under-represented in the survey sample. This may be because the nature of cases at Crown Court are more distressing and therefore witnesses were more reluctant to take part in the research.

It is important to compare the profile of the samples at phase 1 and phase 2, as this can affect interpretation of trend results. In the large part, the profiles matched closely. There were some regional differences although this may be caused by the higher number of courts' recruiting sample in phase 2, which could have changed the regional profile. In terms of categories of vulnerability, there was an increase in the proportion of child witness (from 34% to 42%). The other significant difference is in the proportion of Crown and magistrates' witnesses. In phase 1, 62 per cent of VIWs were from the Crown Court compared with only 43 per cent in phase 2. This can be largely explained by the increased representation of magistrates' courts in the phase 2 sample, which as explained above is likely to be due to Witness Services in magistrates' courts being more efficiently run and better staffed compared with the case in phase 1. In phase 1, only 48 out of the 94 magistrates' courts approached the recruited sample. In phase 2, this rose to 67 out of 94 magistrates' courts. The corresponding increase in the representation of Crown Courts was much lower (from 62 out of 86 in phase 1, to 71 in phase 2) which explains why such a higher proportion of magistrates' court witnesses were included in the phase 2 sample.

Response rate at phase 1

The full response details are given in the table below.

n total, forms for 1,234 witnesses were received from the participating courts, of whom 806 had agreed to be interviewed by BMRB. A further 21 addressees were removed because they were ineligible (e.g. no vulnerabilities identified) or there were insufficient address or other contact details.

Table A.2: Fieldwork response rate (phase 1)

	No of cases	Per cent
Sample issued	785	100%
Ineligible	84	9%
Expert/police	2	*
No verdict	81	8%
Claimed never witness	1	*
Deadwood	14	4%
Moved, untraceable	9	3%
Address untraceable	5	2%
Eligible sample	687	100%
Interview	552	80%
Refusal	38	6%
Unable to contact	51	7%
Other unsuccessful	37	5%

* =< 0.5%

Of the 785 issued to field, nine per cent were found to be further ineligible, mostly because no verdict had been reached in the case and it was agreed with the project steering group that witnesses would not be interviewed until the case was completed. Another four per cent were "deadwood", that is the supplied address was incorrect or the witness had moved and could not be traced. This left an eligible sample of 687 witnesses, of whom n=552 were interviewed between November 2000 – February 2001. Only six per cent of the eligible sample refused to be interviewed.

The response rate based on all addresses in–scope was 80 per cent.

Response at phase 2

In phase 2, 1,737 VIWs were approached, of whom 883 agreed to be interviewed. However, 90 of these cases were removed from the sample as they were ineligible (mainly because they had no witness vulnerabilities). Thus 793 were issued to the fieldforce. After removing 55 cases which were not covered by the end of fieldwork, and 38 ineligible/deadwood, the final number of achieved interviews was 569, a net response rate of 81 per cent.

Table A.3: Fieldwork response rate (phase 2)

	No of cases	Per cent
Sample issued	793	100%
Not covered	55	7%
Ineligible	20	3%
Expert/police	5	1%
No verdict	14	2%
Claimed never witness	1	*
Deadwood	18	2%
Moved, untraceable	14	2%
Address untraceable	4	1%
Eligible sample	700	100%
Interview	569	81%
Refusal	39	6%
Unable to contact	44	6%
Other unsuccessful	48	7%

* = < 0.5%

Appendix B   Reasons for non-response from courts at Phase 1

Although the overall response rate was high (particularly considering that vulnerable witnesses might have been expected to be less willing to cooperate), 24 Crown Courts and 46 magistrates' courts did not return recruitment forms on time at phase 1. BMRB contacted all of these courts by telephone in February 2001 to find out the reasons why witness co-ordinators did not return the recruitment forms. Figure B.1 summarises the results.

BMRB managed to speak to 57 of the 70 Witness Services that had failed to return recruitment forms. Three Crown Court witness co-ordinators could not be contacted. In one case this was because the witness co-ordinator was absent throughout February, in the other two cases they left messages on answerphones but did not receive return calls. A higher number (11) of magistrates' court witness co-ordinators could not be contacted. In five cases their telephone number could not be located (despite searching directory enquiries, the internet, and telephoning the relevant magistrates' courts). In four cases BMRB left messages on answerphones but did not receive return calls. In one case the Witness Service had been merged with another, and in the remaining case the telephone number given rang without answer (on five occasions spread over three weeks).

Those witness coordinators who were successfully contacted were asked if they remembered receiving information from BMRB about the vulnerable witnesses survey. If required, the interviewers prompted their memory by describing the forms and documents that were sent to them and reminding them that the survey was mentioned in the Victim Support newsletter.

Fourteen of the 57 Witness Services BMRB spoke to did not recall receiving any information about the survey. This could be related to problems at either end in ensuring that the forms arrived with the relevant witness co-ordinator. Notably 12 of these Witness Services operated out of magistrates' courts where offices were (at the time of the fieldwork) open less often than Crown Court Witness Service offices. In two cases the witness co-ordinator was new and had started after December 2000: these co-ordinators were completely unaware of the survey.

Figure B.1:   Summary of Witness Service re-contact procedure

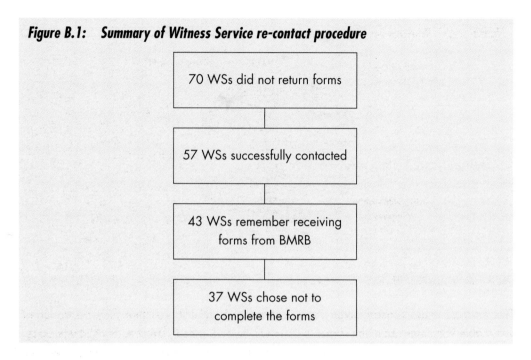

70 WSs did not return forms

57 WSs successfully contacted

43 WSs remember receiving forms from BMRB

37 WSs chose not to complete the forms

BMRB also checked with witness co-ordinators if they had returned recruitment forms. Despite BMRB's records showing otherwise, six courts claimed to have returned the recruitment forms to us. In one of these cases the relevant forms were tracked down at BMRB, but in the remaining five cases it was assumed the forms were not actually sent or were lost in the post.

Reasons for non-return of recruitment forms

Finally we asked the remaining 37 Witness Services the reasons why they chose not to return recruitment forms to BMRB. Figure B.2 illustrates the various reasons given by Witness Services for not returning the recruitment forms to BMRB.

Figure B.2: Reasons for non-return

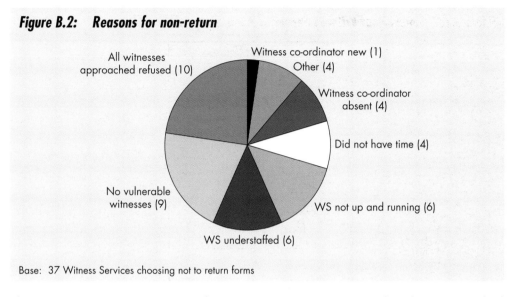

Base: 37 Witness Services choosing not to return forms

The most common reason given (by 10 Witness Services) was that they approached vulnerable witnesses about the survey but the witnesses (or the in the case of child witnesses, the parents or guardian) refused to take part in the survey. For the 10 Witness Services giving this reason, BMRB asked roughly how many vulnerable witnesses were approached. The average number given approached was 6.4, ranging from one refusal by a witness to 30 refusals at a single court.

Nine witness co-ordinators said that no vulnerable witnesses were available during the survey period. They often told BMRB that they operated in smaller courts where serious cases involving vulnerable witnesses were infrequent. Other reasons mainly related to lack of time and understaffing or the newness of the Witness Service for that court. The remainder related to other problems: one claimed that the forms were lost by the previous Witness Co-ordinator, so although the new co-ordinator was aware of the survey, he did not receive the relevant recruitment forms. Another Witness Service was closed for repairs during the survey period and one Witness Service returned the forms, but after the deadline had passed. Only one did not return recruitment forms because it felt the cases involved were very sensitive and the witnesses were too vulnerable to take part in a survey.

References

Angle, H., Malam, S. and Carey, C. (2003). *Key findings from the witness satisfaction survey.* Home Office Research Findings No.189. London: Home Office.

Home Office (1998). *Speaking up for justice.* Report of the Interdepartmental Working Group on the Treatment of Vulnerable or Intimidated Witnesses in the Criminal Justice System. London: Home Office.

Home Office (2003). *Improving Public Satisfaction and Confidence in the Criminal Justice System. Framework Document.* Confidence Task Force (National Criminal Justice Board). London: Home Office.

Kitchen, S. and Elliott, R. (2001). *Key findings from the vulnerable witness survey.* Research Finding No.147. London: Home Office.

Whitehead, E. (2000). *Witness Satisfaction: findings from the Witness Satisfaction Survey 2000.* Home Office Research Study No.230. London: Home Office

RDS Publications

Requests for Publications

Copies of our publications and a list of those currently available may be obtained from:

> Home Office
> Research, Development and Statistics Directorate
> Communication Development Unit
> Room 264, Home Office
> 50 Queen Anne's Gate
> London SW1H 9AT
> Telephone: 020 7273 2084 (answerphone outside of office hours)
> Facsimile: 020 7222 0211
> E-mail: publications.rds@homeoffice.gsi.gov.uk

alternatively

why not visit the RDS web-site at
>   Internet: http://www.homeoffice.gov.uk/rds/index.htm

where many of our publications are available to be read on screen or downloaded for printing.